D1480584

MUFFINS
AND **BISCUITS**

MUFFINS AND BISCUITS

50 RECIPES TO START YOUR DAY WITH A SMILE

Heidi Gibson

photographs BY **ANTONIS ACHILLEOS**

CHRONICLE BOOKS

SAN FRANCISCO

Library of Congress Cataloging-in-Publication Data
Names: Gibson, Heidi, 1972- author. | Achilleos, Antonis,
photographer.
Title: Muffins & biscuits : 50 recipes to start your day with
a smile / Heidi
    Gibson ; photographs by Antonis Achilleos.
Other titles: Muffins and biscuits
Description: San Francisco : Chronicle Books, [2017] |
Includes index.
Identifiers: LCCN 2016021108 | ISBN 9781452158259 (hc
: alk. paper)
Subjects: LCSH: Muffins. | Biscuits. | LCGFT: Cookbooks.
Classification: LCC TX770.M83 G53 2017 | DDC
641.81/57—dc23 LC record available at https://lccn.loc.
gov/2016021108

Manufactured in China

Designed by **VANESSA DINA**
Prop styling by **SPORK**
Typesetting by **FRANK BRAYTON**

Chronicle books and gifts are available at special
quantity discounts to corporations, professional
associations, literacy programs, and other organizations.
For details and discount information, please contact
our premiums department at corporatesales@
chroniclebooks.com or at 1-800-759-0190.

10 9 8 7 6 5 4 3 2 1

Chronicle Books LLC
680 Second Street
San Francisco, California 94107
www.chroniclebooks.com

CONTENTS

MUFFINS 24

BISCUITS 96

BUTTERS AND SPREADS 148

I LOVE MUFFINS AND BISCUITS!

I've been making muffins and biscuits since I was seven years old. As soon as I could read my mother's cookbooks, I tore through them like they were romance novels (which, for me, they were), astonished by the range of what I could make just by following the directions. Muffins were my first love: so easy, with nearly instant gratification, and so many varieties! My vivid childhood memories of making (and eating) muffins have been the inspiration for many of the recipes in this book. I used to make what I called surprise muffins, which come with a spoonful of jam hidden in the middle, and they helped me develop the recipe for my Peanut Butter and Jelly Muffins (page 63). Donut Muffins, plain muffins rolled in melted butter and cinnamon sugar while still warm, were a revelation. So rich, sweet, and fragrant, they are almost sinful, and I now serve them for dessert instead of breakfast. Muffins are a baking rite of passage: they're so easy to make and so rewarding to eat, they make you think you can produce a full array of bakery-quality pastries at home. I eventually moved on to biscuits, cakes, and pies, and later, as a teenager, I even had a fling with choux pastry, which resulted in elaborate towers of profiteroles and cream puffs at family dinners. But I always came back to my first love—muffins.

My mother has recounted for me the story of her first stab at baking biscuits numerous times. As a new bride in her early twenties, she baked some biscuits that became the joke of the marriage. They were so hard, flat, and tasteless that both she and my dad burst out laughing and actually played catch with them at the dinner table instead of eating them. She's been an excellent home baker as long as I can remember (her sticky buns are legendary and her challah once won first place at the state fair), and I was always skeptical of this story, but it has stuck with me. Biscuits are so simple, how could anyone go so astray?

I made it my mission to understand the chemistry and physics of biscuits so that I could make the flakiest, fluffiest, and tastiest ones possible. I've made hundreds, probably thousands, of batches of biscuits trying to master the art of biscuit making. In my quest I've discovered the great variations in biscuit styles and how attached people are to their family recipe. In a few cases, folks have admitted to me that they don't even like their family biscuit recipe, but nostalgia or loyalty compels them to continue using it anyway. Biscuits, for a lot of us, are like that: they have a history, a universal appeal, an almost primitive connection from having been passed down through generations. I also have yet to find anyone who doesn't like biscuits. Sure, some folks

prefer fluffy, some prefer flaky, but everyone loves a good, warm, buttery biscuit. My goal with this book is to explore some of the many traditional styles of biscuit to help all of you establish your own family traditions with your favorites.

My husband, Nate, and I own a restaurant, The American Grilled Cheese Kitchen, and a few months after we opened, we added breakfast to the menu. I have to admit that the decision to do so was as much based on my desire to start baking muffins every day as it was on sound business logic. Fortunately, our regulars liked the muffins as much as I did, and I had a lot of fun coming up with new filling combinations for our customers to try; the best of those experiments are in this book. We added biscuits to the breakfast lineup a couple of months after that, and they were an instant hit. Customers in a hurry could get a fresh biscuit to munch on while heading to the office, or in a couple of extra minutes we could send them on their way with a warm egg-and-cheese biscuit sandwich.

We now serve a variety of from-scratch, freshly baked muffins and biscuits every day at The American Grilled Cheese Kitchen. We use the Perfectly Easy Cream Biscuit recipe (page 99), because it's easy, fast, and delicious, and anyone in the kitchen can make it; it's pretty much foolproof and takes just minutes. We make batches throughout the day, so that the biscuits are always fresh. At home I like to shake it up and make different biscuit styles for different meals or occasions. After spending months testing and retesting the recipes

for this book, Angel Biscuits (page 105) have become my go-to biscuit recipe at home when I'm able to plan a day ahead. The dough comes together nearly as quickly as that for the Cream Biscuits and then sits overnight so that the yeast can do its magic. I can pop them in the oven while preparing the rest of the meal and have one less detail to stress over while pulling together dinner.

Home bakers, especially beginners, will appreciate how friendly muffins and biscuits are. They require no special equipment, training, or expertise and a minimum amount of elbow grease. In fact, the less you mix the batter and handle the dough, the better. They're rustic and homey, and popular with people of all ages. There is, in my humble opinion, nothing else quite like them in their universal appeal and accessibility in the world of traditional American cuisine. I hope you discover something that surprises or delights you in this book and that you try a technique or recipe you use for years to come.

BAKING BASICS

As I mentioned, you don't need much to turn out perfectly delicious muffins and biscuits. A muffin pan, a baking sheet, a couple of bowls, two knives, a spoon, some measuring cups, and an oven will get you there; everything else is optional. You likely have the basic ingredients in your kitchen already: flour, sugar, baking powder, milk, butter, an egg or two. You can stick with the basics or go as wild as you want from there.

INGREDIENTS AND SUBSTITUTIONS

Baking Powder and Baking Soda:
I often use a combination of baking powder and baking soda in these recipes, but sometimes just one or the other—it depends on the rest of the ingredients in the recipe. Baking soda needs to react with something acidic for it to do its thing, so you'll see it used in recipes with buttermilk, lemon juice, and other acidic ingredients. Baking powder has the acidic component built in and is used primarily in recipes lacking an acidic ingredient. Buy double-acting baking powder, such as Calumet or Clabber Girl, as it will give you the best results. Baking soda has a tendency to clump, so use a fork to break up any chunks before measuring it into the flour. Baking powder and baking soda will lose potency over time, so check the expiration date and get new packages if yours have expired.

Bananas:
If you have overripe bananas, don't toss them out. Peel and store them in a resealable plastic bag in the freezer until you're ready to use them. I've never encountered a banana that's too ripe for baking—it's okay if the skin is almost totally black—and bananas actually get sweeter after they've been frozen and thawed.

Butter:
In muffins, butter serves two important functions: it helps prevent the development of gluten, which keeps your muffins tender, and it adds flavor. You can use either salted or unsalted butter for muffins; because there are

only a few tablespoons of butter used, you are unlikely to notice much difference in flavor in the baked muffins. I call for salted butter in these recipes just because it's more likely that you already have some in your refrigerator. To make dairy-free muffins, substitute margarine or a neutral-flavored vegetable oil, such as canola, without making any other adjustments.

For biscuits, many traditional recipes call for lard or shortening, but I prefer the flavor and texture you get from using butter. Biscuits contain a higher percentage of butter than muffins do, so I call for unsalted butter in the biscuit recipes; the amount of salt in salted butter varies by brand and I want to be able to control the amount of salt and get the flavor just right. However, if you want to use salted butter, reduce the salt called for in the recipe by ½ teaspoon. You can substitute vegetable shortening for any or all of the butter in these recipes and follow the recipe as if you were using butter. Solid unrefined coconut oil makes outstanding biscuits, but it will impart a distinct coconut flavor. Whatever fat you use, it should be solid and firm, so portion out what you need and then chill in the refrigerator before starting the recipe, unless directed otherwise.

Eggs:

In addition to helping muffins and biscuits rise, these natural leavening agents lend flavor and structure. You can use egg whites or vegan egg substitute instead of whole eggs in all recipes calling for whole eggs. The average egg is about ¼ cup [50 g]. Use the same total volume of substitute.

Flour:

I use all-purpose flour for almost all of my muffins and biscuits, and I developed these recipes using Bob's Red Mill and King Arthur brands of unbleached all-purpose flour. You are welcome to substitute whole-wheat pastry flour for up to half of the all-purpose flour. The baked goods will be a little heavier and will have a distinct whole-wheat flavor, but they will be delicious nonetheless. White whole-wheat flour or whole-grain spelt flour can also be used for up to three-quarters of the all-purpose flour, and you'll have slightly heavy, but fantastic, results. Gluten-free baking mixes, such as Cup4Cup, can be substituted according to the manufacturer's instructions. Do not use straight gluten-free flour; it will not have the binders that help muffins and biscuits hold together and rise properly. For biscuits with traditional Southern flair, use flour made from soft red winter wheat if you are able to find it—White Lily and Southern Biscuit are two brands to look for—in place of the all-purpose flour and/or cake flour. You can also use self-rising flour; just omit the baking powder and baking soda and use half the salt.

Dairy:

Almost all of these recipes call for whole milk, buttermilk, or sour cream. Milk and other dairy products add moisture, flavor, and, in some cases, acidity to activate baking soda for leavening action. The fat in whole-fat dairy

products helps keep baked goods tender by preventing the development of gluten and also adds a rich mouthfeel to the final product. You are welcome to use nonfat or low-fat milk in place of the whole milk or to substitute soy, almond, cashew, or any other dairy-free "milk." Be aware that many brands of dairy-free milk are sweetened. Rather than try to estimate by how much you need to reduce the amount of sugar in the recipe to compensate, look for dairy-free milk that is unsweetened.

Buttermilk, the liquid left over from making butter, is a magical ingredient in baked goods. The sourness imparts a fuller flavor to both muffins and biscuits, and the acidity reacts with baking soda to make carbon dioxide, which helps make biscuits fluffy. Use traditional low-fat or cultured full-fat (Bulgarian) buttermilk, whichever is more easily available, in any of these recipes. If you don't have buttermilk handy, you can make "soured" milk: spoon 1 tablespoon of lemon juice or white vinegar into a measuring cup and then add enough milk to make 1 cup [240 ml]. Let the liquid sit for 5 minutes before using. The "soured-milk" technique also works on unsweetened nondairy milk. You can also mix equal parts of plain yogurt or sour cream and milk and substitute the mixture for the buttermilk.

Crème fraîche or plain yogurt may be substituted for sour cream. You are welcome to use low-fat or nonfat sour cream or yogurt; the flavor will be a bit less rich but you will still have a fine result.

Nuts:

Walnuts, almonds, pecans, pistachios, coconuts, and pine nuts are used in recipes throughout this book. Nuts add flavor, texture, aroma, and visual appeal. In all cases, nuts benefit from toasting before being used in muffins or biscuits: toasting intensifies the flavor and crunch. The only time you don't want to toast nuts before using for these recipes is when you're adding nuts to streusel, because the nuts will toast in the oven as the muffins bake.

To toast nuts, spread them in a single layer on a baking sheet and bake in a preheated 350°F [180°C] oven until they are barely browned and emit a fragrant, nutty aroma. Watch carefully and check every minute after the first 4 minutes to prevent burning. Immediately pour them onto a plate to cool. Note that chopped or sliced nuts will toast faster than whole nuts.

Almonds, pine nuts, and pistachios	4 to 8 minutes
Walnuts and pecans	5 to 10 minutes
Coconut flakes or shreds	3 to 5 minutes

Yeast:

Occasionally I use active dry yeast (see Angel Biscuits, page 105), often in addition to baking powder and baking soda. Keep yeast in the refrigerator and check the expiration date; discard any yeast that has expired. Many recipes call for proofing yeast (mixing it with warm water or milk and a little sugar until it bubbles) before adding it to dough, but proofing isn't necessary with modern commercial yeast, which is highly unlikely to be inactive if used before the expiration date. If you keep yeast in the refrigerator and discard any that has expired, then you can mix dry yeast right into the flour for all recipes calling for yeast.

Fruit:
If the fruit is going to be baked, it really doesn't matter if you use fresh or frozen fruit. In fact, unless you're getting in-season fruit at the farmers' market, frozen fruit, which is picked and flash-frozen at the height of ripeness, is often more flavorful than fresh. For fresh berries, rinse, pat dry, and pick them over to remove any debris or moldy berries before using. For fresh stone fruit, you'll get the best results with ripe, fragrant fruit that is still a bit firm, but there's no need to discard any soft or bruised bits. Although it is usually unnecessary, you can peel stone fruit if you wish (it's much easier to peel fruit that is still fairly firm), but I don't bother peeling stone fruit for muffins, which are meant to be rustic and homey. If peeling is required, it will be specified in the recipe.

MEASURING

The easiest and most accurate way to measure dry ingredients is to weigh them on a scale. And, as a bonus, you can measure directly into the bowl on the scale and wind up with fewer dishes to wash! Look for a scale that measures both ounces and grams and can accommodate at least 5 pounds [2.3 kg]. I personally recommend buying a digital scale; it's easier to use and read.

If you don't have a scale, measure dry ingredients like flour using the "dip, level, pour" technique. First, dip your dry measuring cup or spoon into the flour, baking powder, sugar, etc., so that the cup is overfull, then run the back of a flat dinner knife across the surface of the cup to remove the excess and pour into a mixing bowl. Always use "dry" measures (cups that you fill to the brim and can level off) for dry ingredients like flour and sugar; use "wet" measures (clear containers with marks on the side so you can see how high you're filling the container) for wet ingredients like milk.

CUTTING IN

This technique is used to prepare biscuits and some of the streusel toppings for the muffins. For the best results, most recipes require that you "cut in" the butter or other fat. This ensures even distribution of tiny solid bits of fat throughout the flour mixture; when these bits of fat melt in the oven, they create flaky, tender layers. The following four alternative techniques will produce perfect biscuits if properly employed. Always start with very cold butter or fat and always whisk your dry ingredients together thoroughly to eliminate any clumps of baking soda, sugar, or anything else before you start to cut in.

Rubbing:
Toss the chunks of cold butter with the flour mixture and then rub the butter chunks between your thumb and fingers to break up the butter and coat it thoroughly with flour. Stop when the dough resembles coarse wet sand and there are still some small visible chunks of butter.

Two Knives:

Toss chunks of cold butter into the flour mixture and then, holding a dinner knife in each hand, point them business-end-down into the mixture and pull the knives away from each other repeatedly to cut the butter into smaller pieces. Stop when the dough resembles coarse wet sand and there are still some small visible chunks of butter.

Pastry Cutter or Pastry Blender:

Toss chunks of cold butter into the flour mixture and then press a pastry cutter (a small handheld device made especially for cutting butter into dough) straight down into the mixture repeatedly, stirring occasionally to make sure you're cutting evenly, until the mixture resembles coarse wet sand and there are still some small visible chunks of butter.

Food Processor:

As far as small kitchen appliances go, the food processor is one of the absolute handiest; it makes cutting in fat as easy as pressing a lever. Once you have fitted the processor with the metal blade attachment, you can measure all the dry ingredients directly into the bowl and pulse for a few seconds to mix them. Then toss in the cold fat and pulse to cut it in. Five 1-second pulses works for my processor, but everyone's machine is a little different, so watch yours carefully to figure out what the ideal time is for your machine. Checking after each 1-second pulse will prevent you from overmixing. When I'm feeling really lazy about washing dishes and have room in my freezer, I'll put the processor bowl on the scale (with the blade inside), weigh dry ingredients directly into the bowl, mix the dry ingredients in the processor for a couple of pulses, remove the bowl (still leaving the blade inside), toss in the butter, and just put the whole bowl in the freezer for about 10 minutes before continuing.

MUFFIN BASICS

Muffins are very easy to prepare, but here are a few tips to keep in mind to make sure that you get the best results.

MIXING THE BATTER

For the muffins in this book, follow my strategy of whisking the dry ingredients together thoroughly in one medium bowl, whisking the wet ingredients together thoroughly in a separate large bowl, then adding the dry ingredients to the wet ingredients and just barely folding them together along with whatever fillings you may be adding. This oh-so-gentle final folding of wet and dry ingredients guarantees you will have muffins that are as tender and light as possible. Make sure you do not overmix the batter. You will know at a glance when you pull the muffins out of the oven if you have overdone it. Instead of each muffin having a gently round dome, peaks will form as they bake, and instead of the tiny imperceptible air pockets that a perfectly baked muffin should have, long vertical air tunnels will form inside, sure signs your muffins will be tough (but they'll still make a fantastic bread pudding! See the recipe on page 95). There's

no fix once you have overmixed the batter; just remember to use a lighter hand next time. I like to use a wire whisk for mixing the wet and dry ingredients separately, and then I use a rubber spatula to fold them together (the rubber spatula is also handy for scraping out those last bits of delicious batter).

A quick note on mixing in sugar: traditionally sugar is mixed in with the wet ingredients rather than the dry ingredients. I generally call for mixing white granulated sugar with the dry ingredients because I find that it makes the flour mixture easier to fold into the wet ingredients. However, brown sugar tends to clump and is more difficult to mix thoroughly into flour, so I recommend mixing brown sugar with the wet ingredients.

TO LINE OR NOT TO LINE?

Paper muffin liners can be helpful in a number of ways, particularly when the time comes to get the muffins out of the pan. Decorative liners can dress up muffins and make them look impressive, and they encourage fluffier muffins by giving the batter a nice paper surface to climb up as they rise in the oven. I'm particularly fond of tulip baking cups, which are folded paper squares placed into the wells. These extend out from the top of the muffin cups and prevent the batter from overflowing, so you don't have to worry about overfilling the wells. They also look fantastic, as though your muffins came out of a high-end French bakery. I also have a set of silicone muffin liners and a silicone muffin pan that I use regularly at home; they are the ultimate in nonstick baking utensils and make cleanup a breeze, plus you don't have to remember to buy paper liners.

For a few recipes, I advise against using liners, because those particular muffins (such as Fresh Corn and Masa Muffins with Bacon and Jalapeños on page 83 and Cider–Corn Bread Muffins on page 86) are better with a nice brown crust and liners inhibit crust formation. If you are not using liners, be sure to spray or butter the wells thoroughly to prevent the muffins from sticking to the insides of the wells.

MUFFIN SIZES AND BAKING

With the muffin recipes in this book, you can use almost any size muffin pan, including jumbo, regular, mini, and really-really-mini, as well as pans for muffin tops, tea loaves, novelty shapes, and even popovers. I've given baking instructions for the most common sizes—regular and jumbo—in the recipes. For other sizes and shapes, here are some rough baking guidelines. It's always a good idea, however, to watch your muffins carefully to avoid overbaking them.

- Do not adjust the temperature for different sizes; adjust the time.
- Whatever size wells or pan you are using, fill about three-fourths full, not all the way to the top (unless otherwise specified in the recipe), to prevent the batter from overflowing in the oven. Streusel can be piled on top of the batter; it's okay if it is mounded over the top of the wells or the pan.

- Bake muffins in the center of a preheated oven. If your oven has a convection setting, make sure that it is turned on. If you are baking two or more pans of muffins at the same time, switch their position when you rotate the pans halfway through baking to ensure they bake evenly.
- Muffins are done when the tops are puffed and rounded and they bounce back when you gently poke them in the center of the top with a finger. If in doubt, check for doneness by poking a sharp knife or skewer into the center of a muffin. If it comes out clean, the muffins are done.
- Mini muffins will be done 5 to 7 minutes *before* the required time for regular muffins.
- Mini loaf breads (which usually have 2-by-4-inch [5-by-10-cm] to 3-by-5-inch [7.5-by-12-cm] wells) will be done in about the same time as jumbo muffins, but may take 3 to 5 minutes more.

STORING MUFFINS

As with most baked goods that are not loaded with undesirable preservatives, proper storage is important and in some cases can lengthen their short shelf life. Here are some suggestions that have worked for me.

Muffins:

I think muffins are best when they are consumed within 2 hours of their leaving the oven. If you want to, however, you can store them at room temperature (they will go stale faster if you refrigerate them) for up to two days. Let the muffins cool completely first, then place them in a resealable container. Before serving, refresh them in a preheated 350°F [180°C] oven for 3 to 5 minutes, or just until warmed through (you can put the muffins back in the muffin pan or set them on a baking sheet). If you want to store the muffins for more than two days, wrap them tightly in plastic wrap or place them in a resealable bag, and then freeze them for up to one month. When you are ready to serve them, remove the plastic wrap and put them in a preheated 350°F [180°C] oven for 5 to 7 minutes, or until warmed through. I recommend against rewarming muffins in a microwave.

Muffin Batter:

If you want to get things started ahead of time, make the batter, cover the bowl tightly with plastic wrap (or divide equally among the muffin cups and then wrap the muffin pan with plastic wrap), and refrigerate for up to two days before baking. If the recipe calls for any streusel or other kind of topping, do not add it until right before the muffins go into the oven; otherwise, the topping on the baked muffin will be soggy instead of crunchy. You can prepare and store streusel in a separate resealable container in the refrigerator for up to one month.

BISCUIT BASICS

HANDLING BISCUIT DOUGH

In this book I use a variety of techniques for mixing, kneading, and rolling because I want to help novice biscuit makers determine which style and technique they prefer and learn how different processes lead to very different results. With all of these recipes, the goal is tall, light, and tender biscuits, and there are a few universal truths to keep in mind.

Keep It Cold:

Little chunks of butter (or, in the case of Ultra-Flaky Biscuits [page 107], thin sheets of butter) will melt while the biscuit bakes and create delicious layers; the steam from the water in the butter will help the biscuits rise. To ensure little unmelted chunks of butter remain, keep the ingredients and dough at room temperature or colder from beginning to end. If it's hot in your kitchen, try putting all the dry ingredients along with the fat (unless you're using coconut oil; it will turn rock-hard in a freezer, so just refrigerate it) in the freezer for 10 minutes before you start, and keep the liquids in the refrigerator until you need them. If you sense that your dough is getting warm, just cover it and put it in the fridge for 10 minutes before proceeding.

Use a Light Hand:

Less is (usually) more when it comes to biscuits. To keep the biscuits very tender, handle the dough as little as possible.

Give Your Biscuits a Rest:

I call for "resting" the dough in many of these recipes. This may seem like a waste of time, but resting dough can be an important step; it allows the liquid to be distributed more evenly through the flour (so less mixing and handling are required) and will lead to a more consistent shape and texture in the finished biscuits. I skip it in recipes where the shape of the final biscuit is rough and simplicity is at a premium, such as Perfectly Easy Cream Biscuits (page 99) and Cathead Biscuits (page 101).

CUTTING BISCUITS

Round, square, dainty bite-size, or as big as your head . . . you can adjust the size and shape of all the biscuits in this book. If you choose to make your biscuits larger or smaller than the sizes called for, remember to adjust the baking time and keep a close eye on your biscuits in the oven. For recipes that require cutting the biscuits, I recommend you use one of the following two techniques.

Biscuit Cutter:

Patting with your hands from the center out, or rolling with a pin, form the dough into a round disk ¾ to 1 inch [2 to 2.5 cm] thick. Use a clean, dry biscuit cutter dipped in flour between each cut. Push the cutter straight down without twisting. Cut as many biscuits as you can from the disk of dough. Gently gather the scraps, reroll, trying to handle the dough as little as possible, and cut additional biscuits. The first biscuits are always prettier than the last ones; nothing you can do about that.

Sharp Knife:

Patting with your hands from the center out, or rolling with a pin, form the dough into a square ¾ to 1 inch [2 to 2.5 cm] thick. Dipping the knife in flour between each cut, trim about ¼ to ½ inch [6 to 12 mm] of dough from the edges of the square so that you have nice sharp edges and then cut the remaining dough into evenly sized squares. You can form the scraps cut off the edges into one more biscuit. This technique has the advantage of leaving fewer scraps to reroll, plus you can cut the biscuits to whatever size you like.

BAKING BISCUITS

High temperatures, usually 400° to 500°F [200° to 260°C], are needed to get biscuits that are brown and crisp on the outside and soft and fluffy on the inside. For recipes using more sugar, I call for lower temperatures, around 375°F [190°C]. Sugar causes the biscuits to brown faster, so the edges can burn before the middle is done if they are baked at a higher temperature. A few tips:

- If your oven has a convection setting, then definitely use it for all biscuit recipes. Let your oven come fully up to temperature before putting the biscuits in. If your oven doesn't have a built-in thermometer, then I recommend buying a small oven thermometer so that you'll know when your oven is ready.
- Parchment paper is the ideal baking sheet lining, and I recommend investing in a roll of it for baking (it's great for baking cookies, too). It will prevent the biscuits from sticking to the sheet, and there will be no burnt bits on the bottoms. It also makes cleanup a breeze. If you don't have parchment paper, then give a clean, dry baking sheet a light coating of nonstick spray and place the biscuits directly on the baking sheet.
- Bake biscuits in the center of the oven, and rotate the pan once halfway through baking to ensure even browning.
- If the biscuits are evenly golden brown and puffed, they're done; no need to use a cake tester to check them.
- Let the biscuits cool on the pan on a wire rack for about 5 minutes and then serve them as quickly as possible; they are best fresh from the oven.

STORING BISCUITS

If you have leftover biscuits, wrap them well (I like to put them in a resealable plastic bag) and keep them at room temperature for up to two days or put them in the freezer for up to a month. Either way, you should "refresh" them before serving by putting them back on a baking sheet (no need to grease it) and in a preheated 400°F [200°C] oven (or toaster oven) for 2 to 3 minutes if starting from room temperature or about 5 minutes if starting from frozen. You can also microwave frozen biscuits for about 15 seconds to thaw before refreshing them in the oven for 2 to 3 minutes.

STREUSEL BASICS

Sweet, crunchy streusel adds a touch of decadence to your muffins. Start with very cold butter (you can even freeze it after cutting while you measure out the dry ingredients if it's warm in your kitchen) and don't overwork it: you want to cut the butter into the flour and sugar without it melting, so that it bakes into nice crunchy little chunks. Streusel is always optional, but it's so easy to make and produces such rewarding results, why not take a minute and whip some up? It's also very flexible: you can toss in some chopped nuts, seeds, or coconut flakes to change up the flavor and texture. This is the most basic version, but I call for variations throughout the book to enhance and decorate muffins in complementary ways.

BASIC STREUSEL

MAKES ABOUT ¾ CUP [135 G]

⅓ cup [45 g] all-purpose flour

3½ Tbsp firmly packed brown sugar

2½ Tbsp cold salted butter, cut into ½-in [12-mm] pieces

In the bowl of a food processor fitted with the metal blade, pulse the flour and brown sugar once or twice until mixed. Cut in the butter with 1-second pulses until the streusel just starts to clump together and visible butter chunks are no bigger than pea-size. (Alternatively, combine the butter, flour, and brown sugar in a bowl and use two knives or rub between your fingers to break up the butter into pea-size pieces.) The streusel should be a mixture of crumbly and chunky. Store in a resealable container in the refrigerator for up to 2 weeks.

MUFFINS

YUMMO!

BAKE-SALE BERRY
MUFFINS

MAKES 12 REGULAR OR 6 JUMBO MUFFINS

Have you ever wondered how the blueberry muffins in bakeries get to look so perfect, with no purple patches or soggy berry blobs on the bottom? The trick is to layer the berries into the muffin cups instead of stirring them into the batter. In this recipe, use almost any combination of fresh or frozen summer fruits—berries, stone fruits, even rhubarb (technically a vegetable)—and your muffins will come out picture perfect every time.

6 Tbsp [85 g] salted butter, melted and cooled

2 eggs

⅓ cup [80 ml] whole milk

1 tsp vanilla extract

1⅓ cups [180 g] all-purpose flour

¾ cup [150 g] sugar

1½ tsp baking powder

½ tsp kosher salt

2 cups [280 g] berries or other fruit

1 recipe Basic Streusel (page 23)

1) Preheat the oven to 350°F [180°C]. Line a 12-well standard or 6-well jumbo muffin pan with paper liners or coat thoroughly with nonstick cooking spray.

2) In a large bowl, whisk together the melted butter and the eggs. Add the milk and vanilla and whisk until well combined. In a medium bowl, whisk together the flour, sugar, baking powder, and salt.

3) Add the flour mixture to the butter mixture and carefully fold together with a rubber spatula until just combined. Be careful not to overmix, or your muffins will be tough; the batter should still have a couple of streaks of flour.

4) Spoon about 1 Tbsp of batter (2 Tbsp for jumbo muffins) into each prepared muffin well. Using half of the berries, sprinkle the batter in each well with an equal amount of berries. Using half of the remaining batter, top the berries with an equal amount of batter. Sprinkle the remaining berries as before and top each well with an equal amount of the remaining batter. Mound the streusel evenly over the top of each filled well.

CONT'D

5) Bake until the tops are golden brown and a muffin bounces back when you poke it gently in the center with a finger, 22 to 26 minutes for standard size or 30 to 35 minutes for jumbo.

6) Remove the muffins from the oven and let cool in the pan for 5 to 10 minutes. Carefully lift the muffins from the pan and transfer them to a wire rack to cool a little more. (Use a butter knife, if needed, to lift the muffins out if you didn't use paper liners.) Serve warm.

Variations

The sky—or the season—is the limit for the fruits you can use in these flavor-popping layered muffins. Fresh or frozen, or a mix of both, is fine. Don't worry about thawing frozen fruit; it can go straight in. Use whole fruit for small berries (blueberries, blackberries, raspberries), halved or quartered for sour cherries or strawberries, and chunks (about ½ in [12 mm]) for stone fruit (peaches, plums, apricots) or rhubarb (discard the green parts if using fresh rhubarb). If using strawberries, raspberries, or stone fruits, fold the whole amount carefully into the batter at the end of Step 3 instead of creating layers; these fruits will not stain the batter, so you do not need to layer them in.

Very Berry: Use ⅔ cup [90 g] blueberries, ⅔ cup [80 g] raspberries, and ⅔ cup [80 g] blackberries for the fruit.

Berry-Peach: Use 1 cup [140 g] blueberries and 1 cup [140 g] diced ripe peaches for the fruit.

Apricot-Raspberry: Use 1 cup [120 g] raspberries and 1 cup [140 g] diced ripe apricots for the fruit.

Strawberry-Rhubarb: Use 1 cup [140 g] fresh or frozen quartered strawberries and 1 cup [140 g] fresh or frozen rhubarb, cut into ½-in [12-mm] chunks, for the fruit.

Blueberry-Lemon: Use 2 cups [280 g] blueberries for the fruit. Add 2 tsp lemon extract and 1 Tbsp lemon zest to the butter mixture.

BALSAMIC STRAWBERRY
MUFFINS

MAKES 12 REGULAR OR 6 JUMBO MUFFINS

This is one of those recipes that came to me as an epiphany. While I was making the morning muffins for the shop: "We have strawberries. What tastes good with strawberries? Balsamic vinegar!" Your gut reaction might be that vinegar has no place in baked goods, but it's actually fairly common and uncommonly delicious. You get what you pay for with balsamic vinegar, and it's worth it to use a higher quality aged vinegar in this recipe; you will be able to taste the difference. The addition of vinegar changes the chemistry of the batter, and I did some tinkering to get this version to come out just right. The muffins puffed up beautifully in the oven but collapsed once they cooled. After a few experiments in our state-of-the-art food-science laboratory (okay, our home kitchen), I cracked the code. The secret was switching entirely to baking soda and leaving out the baking powder.

6 Tbsp [85 g] salted butter, melted and cooled

2 eggs

⅓ cup [80 ml] whole milk

1 tsp vanilla extract

2 Tbsp balsamic vinegar

1⅓ cups [180 g] all-purpose flour

½ cup [100 g] sugar

½ tsp baking soda

½ tsp kosher salt

2 cups [280 g] fresh or frozen strawberries, cut into ½-in [12-mm] pieces

1 recipe Basic Streusel (page 23)

1) Preheat the oven to 350°F [180°C]. Line a 12-well standard or 6-well jumbo muffin pan with paper liners or coat thoroughly with nonstick cooking spray.

2) In a large bowl, whisk together the melted butter and the eggs. Add the milk, vanilla, and balsamic vinegar and whisk until well combined. In a medium bowl, whisk together the flour, sugar, baking soda, and salt.

3) Add the flour mixture to the butter mixture and use a rubber spatula to carefully fold together until just combined. Gently fold in the strawberries. Be careful not to overmix, or your muffins will be tough; the batter should still have a couple of streaks of flour.

4) Divide the batter equally among the prepared muffin wells and mound the streusel evenly over the top of each filled well.

CONT'D

5) Bake until the tops are golden brown and a muffin bounces back when you poke it gently in the center with a finger, 22 to 26 minutes for standard size or 30 to 35 minutes for jumbo.

6) Remove the muffins from the oven and let them cool in the pan for 5 to 10 minutes. Carefully lift the muffins from the pan and transfer them to a wire rack to cool a little more. (Use a butter knife, if needed, to lift the muffins out if you didn't use paper liners.) Serve warm.

GINGER-PEACH
MUFFINS

MAKES 12 REGULAR OR 6 JUMBO MUFFINS

We have spectacular farmers' markets in San Francisco, and in the summer they are bursting with every kind of stone fruit imaginable: five or six types of fuzzy fragrant peaches, delicate apricots, ten kinds of plums, plus pluots, apriums, and every other stone fruit hybrid around. The smell is intoxicating, and the farmers will let you sample everything. I came up with this recipe after lugging home 10 pounds of perfectly ripe white peaches, which have a gorgeous honeysuckle scent, from the Sunday market a few blocks from my house. If you don't have fresh ginger, don't worry; you can add 2 teaspoons powdered ginger to the dry ingredients in Step 3, but the muffins won't have quite the same spicy kick.

GINGER STREUSEL

2½ Tbsp cold salted butter, cut into ½-in [12-mm] pieces

⅓ cup [45 g] all-purpose flour

3½ Tbsp firmly packed brown sugar

¼ cup [40 g] chopped crystallized ginger

BATTER

6 Tbsp [85 g] salted butter, melted and cooled

2 eggs

⅓ cup [80 ml] whole milk

1 tsp vanilla extract

1 Tbsp peeled and finely grated fresh ginger

1⅓ cups [180 g] all-purpose flour

¾ cup [150 g] granulated sugar

1½ tsp baking powder

½ tsp kosher salt

10 oz [280 g] ripe white or yellow peaches, pitted and cut into ½-in [12-mm] chunks

1) Preheat the oven to 350°F [180°C]. Line a 12-well standard or 6-well jumbo muffin pan with paper liners or coat thoroughly with nonstick cooking spray.

2) To make the streusel: In the bowl of a food processor fitted with the metal blade, pulse the butter, flour, and brown sugar in 1-second intervals until the butter is cut into pea-size pieces. (Alternatively, combine the butter, flour, and brown sugar in a bowl and use two knives or rub between your fingers to break up the butter into pea-size pieces.) Stir in the chopped ginger. The streusel should be a mixture of crumbly and chunky. Set aside.

3) To make the batter: In a large bowl, whisk together the melted butter and the eggs. Add the milk, vanilla, and grated ginger and whisk until well combined. In a medium bowl, whisk together the flour, granulated sugar, baking powder, and salt.

4) Add the flour mixture to the butter mixture and use a rubber spatula to carefully fold together until almost combined. Gently fold the peach chunks into the batter. Be careful not to overmix, or your muffins will be tough; the batter should still have a couple of streaks of flour.

5) Divide the batter equally among the prepared muffin wells and mound the streusel evenly over the top of each filled well.

6) Bake until the tops are golden brown and a muffin bounces back when you poke it gently in the center with a finger, 22 to 26 minutes for standard size or 30 to 35 minutes for jumbo.

7) Remove the muffins from the oven and let cool in the pan for 5 to 10 minutes. Carefully lift the muffins from the pan and transfer them to a wire rack to cool a little more. (Use a butter knife, if needed, to lift the muffins out if you didn't use paper liners.) Serve warm.

Variations

Ginger-Plum: Substitute ripe plums or pluots for the peaches. Whisk ¼ tsp freshly ground nutmeg into the flour mixture in Step 3.

Ginger-Apricot: Substitute ripe apricots or apriums for the peaches.

CRANBERRY-ORANGE MUFFINS
WITH ORANGE GLAZE

MAKES 12 REGULAR OR 6 JUMBO MUFFINS

This terrific flavor combination—a perfect balance of tart cranberries that burst in your mouth and sweet fresh orange—is a big, enlivening morning treat, especially in late fall, when cranberries are in season and widely available in the supermarket. Buy an extra bag, freeze them, and enjoy these muffins all year long. They are just as delicious topped with streusel instead of orange glaze. Omit the glaze and mound the filled muffin wells evenly with one batch of Basic Streusel (page 23) before putting the pan in the oven in Step 5.

1 large thick-skinned orange, such as navel (it's difficult to zest thin-skinned oranges)

6 Tbsp [85 g] salted butter, melted and cooled

2 eggs

2 Tbsp whole milk

1 tsp vanilla extract

2 cups [220 g] fresh or frozen cranberries (do not use dried)

1⅓ cups [180 g] all-purpose flour

¾ cup [150 g] granulated sugar

1½ tsp baking powder

½ tsp kosher salt

½ cup [60 g] confectioners' sugar, plus up to 3 Tbsp more

1) Preheat the oven to 350°F [180°C]. Line a 12-well standard or 6-well jumbo muffin pan with paper liners or coat thoroughly with nonstick cooking spray.

2) Using a microplane-style grater or the smallest holes on a box grater, remove all the zest from the orange, carefully avoiding the bitter white pith underneath the fragrant orange skin. Scrape the zest clinging to the grater into a large bowl. Cut the orange in half and squeeze the juice into a small bowl. Measure 1 Tbsp juice (for the orange glaze) into a separate small bowl and set aside. Measure ¼ cup [60 ml] of the remaining juice and pour it into the large bowl with the zest. Save any extra juice for another use.

3) Whisk the melted butter and eggs into the orange juice mixture. Add the milk and vanilla and whisk until well combined. Add the cranberries to the orange juice mixture and stir to combine. In a medium bowl, whisk together the flour, granulated sugar, baking powder, and salt.

4) Add the flour mixture to the butter mixture and use a rubber spatula to carefully fold together until just combined. Be careful not to overmix, or your muffins will be tough; the batter should still have a couple of streaks of flour.

5) Divide the batter equally among the prepared muffin wells. (If you have opted for streusel, mound it evenly over each filled well.)

6) Bake until the tops are golden brown and a muffin bounces back when you poke it gently in the center with a finger, 22 to 26 minutes for standard size or 30 to 35 minutes for jumbo.

7) While the muffins are baking, prepare a glaze (if not using streusel) by whisking the confectioners' sugar into the reserved 1 Tbsp orange juice until smooth. The glaze should be quite thick, so that if you lift the whisk from the bowl it will run slowly off the end of the whisk in a thick ribbon. If necessary, whisk in additional powdered sugar 1 Tbsp at a time.

8) Remove the muffins from the oven and let cool in the pan for 5 to 10 minutes. Carefully lift the muffins from the pan (use a butter knife to lift the muffins out if you didn't use paper liners) and transfer them to a wire rack to cool to room temperature, at least another 10 minutes. Spoon an equal amount of the prepared glaze evenly over each muffin (you may need to gently spread it over the tops of the muffins with the back of a dinner spoon and it may run down the sides a bit). Allow the glaze to set for 5 minutes before serving.

APRICOT-ALMOND
MUFFINS

MAKES 12 REGULAR OR 6 JUMBO MUFFINS

I grew up in Southern California in a house that was surrounded by fruit trees: apricots, peaches, plums, figs, loquats, persimmons, guavas, and apples. Aside from the guavas, which as a child I did not appreciate and used for target practice (don't worry, I've seen the error of my ways!), I loved them all, but the tart and flavorful Blenheim apricots were my favorite. During the summer, when they ripened, I would climb into the big old tree and eat as many as I could; my mother would use the ones that escaped my clutches to make fruit leather or to cook into jam. I prefer to use dried apricots in this recipe because they have more concentrated flavor than fresh ones. Plus, using dried apricots means I can make these muffins year-round. And, no surprise, I suggest using the Blenheim (California grown) apricots rather than Turkish varieties for this recipe if you can find them.

ALMOND STREUSEL

2½ Tbsp cold salted butter, cut into ½-in [12-mm] pieces

⅓ cup [45 g] all-purpose flour

3½ Tbsp firmly packed brown sugar

⅓ cup [40 g] sliced raw almonds

BATTER

6 Tbsp [85 g] salted butter, melted and cooled

2 eggs

⅓ cup [80 ml] whole milk

2 tsp almond extract

1 tsp vanilla extract

1⅓ cups [185 g] all-purpose flour

⅔ cup [130 g] granulated sugar

1½ tsp baking powder

½ tsp kosher salt

1 cup [120 g] sliced almonds, toasted (see page 15)

8 oz [230 g] dried California or Blenheim apricots, chopped into ½-in [12-mm] pieces, soaked in hot water for 30 minutes, and then drained

1) Preheat the oven to 350°F [180°C]. Line a 12-well standard or 6-well jumbo muffin pan with paper liners or coat thoroughly with nonstick cooking spray.

2) To make the streusel: In the bowl of a food processor fitted with the metal blade, pulse the butter, flour, and brown sugar in 1-second intervals until the butter is cut into pea-size pieces. (Alternatively, combine the butter, flour, and brown sugar in a bowl and use two knives or rub between your fingers to break up the butter into pea-size pieces.) Stir in the raw sliced almonds. The streusel should be a mixture of crumbly and chunky. Set aside.

3) To make the batter: In a large bowl, whisk together the melted butter and the eggs. Add the milk, almond extract, and vanilla and whisk until well combined. In a medium bowl, whisk together the flour, granulated sugar, baking powder, and salt. Stir in the toasted almonds.

4) Add the flour mixture to the butter mixture and use a rubber spatula to carefully fold together until almost combined. Gently fold the apricots into the batter. Be careful not to overmix, or your muffins will be tough; the batter should still have a couple of streaks of flour.

5) Divide the batter equally among the prepared muffin wells and mound each well with an equal amount of the streusel.

6) Bake until the tops are golden brown and a muffin bounces back when you poke it gently in the center with a finger, 22 to 26 minutes for standard size or 30 to 35 minutes for jumbo.

7) Remove the muffins from the oven and let cool in the pan for 5 to 10 minutes. Carefully lift the muffins from the pan and transfer them to a wire rack to cool a little more. (Use a butter knife to lift the muffins out if you didn't use paper liners.) Serve warm.

Variations

Raspberry-Almond: Substitute 2 cups [240 g] whole fresh or frozen raspberries for the dried apricots; skip soaking. Bake as directed.

Plum-Almond: Substitute 8½ oz [240 g] fresh plums, pitted and cut into ½-in [12-mm] chunks, for the dried apricots; skip soaking. Bake as directed.

PIÑA COLADA
MUFFINS

MAKES 12 REGULAR OR 6 JUMBO MUFFINS

That's right! Have a piña colada for breakfast! With the ever-popular flavor combination of pineapple, coconut, and rum (no little paper umbrellas needed), these unique muffins taste as good as they look. The coconut milk reinforces the tropical flavor, but you can use low-fat or whole cow's milk if you don't have any on hand. I use unsweetened coconut flakes, but sweetened works well, too.

COCONUT STREUSEL

2½ Tbsp cold salted butter, cut into ½-in [12-mm] pieces

⅓ cup [45 g] all-purpose flour

3½ Tbsp firmly packed brown sugar

½ cup [40 g] unsweetened raw coconut flakes or shredded sweetened raw coconut

BATTER

6 Tbsp [85 g] salted butter, melted and cooled

2 eggs

6 Tbsp [90 ml] coconut milk, whisked until smooth if there is a layer of coconut oil on top ("lite" coconut milk is fine, too)

1 tsp vanilla extract

2 Tbsp dark rum or 1 tsp rum extract

1½ cups [180 g] all-purpose flour

¾ cup [150 g] granulated sugar

1½ tsp baking powder

½ tsp kosher salt

1½ cups [340 g] drained canned or fresh pineapple chunks

1⅓ cups [120 g] unsweetened coconut flakes, roughly chopped or shredded sweetened coconut, toasted (see page 15)

1) Preheat the oven to 350°F [180°C]. Line a 12-well standard or 6-well jumbo muffin pan with paper liners or coat thoroughly with nonstick cooking spray.

2) To make the streusel: In the bowl of a food processor fitted with the metal blade, pulse the butter, flour, and brown sugar in 1-second intervals until the butter is cut into pea-size pieces. (Alternatively, combine the butter, flour, and brown sugar in a bowl and use two knives or rub between your fingers to break up the butter into pea-size pieces.) Stir in the coconut. The streusel should be a mixture of crumbly and chunky. Set aside.

3) To make the batter: In a large bowl, whisk together the melted butter and the eggs. Add the coconut milk, vanilla, and rum and whisk until well combined. In a medium bowl, whisk together the flour, granulated sugar, baking powder, and salt.

CONT'D

4) Add the flour mixture to the butter mixture and use a rubber spatula to carefully fold together until just combined. Gently fold in the pineapple and coconut. Be careful not to overmix, or your muffins will be tough; the batter should still have a couple of streaks of flour.

5) Divide the batter equally among the prepared muffin wells and mound each well with an equal amount of the streusel.

6) Bake until the tops are golden brown and a muffin bounces back when you poke it gently in the center with a finger, 22 to 26 minutes for standard size or 30 to 35 minutes for jumbo.

7) Remove the muffins from the oven and let cool in the pan for 5 to 10 minutes. Carefully lift the muffins from the pan and transfer them to a wire rack to cool a little more. (Use a butter knife to lift the muffins out if you didn't use paper liners.) Serve warm.

SOUR CREAM– COFFEE CAKE
MUFFINS

MAKES 12 REGULAR OR 6 JUMBO MUFFINS

These muffins feature a classic sour cream–coffee cake base with layers of crunchy cinnamon streusel. The process for making the batter is different from that for most of the other muffins in this book, because I wanted a light but rich cake texture with a finer crumb rather than a traditional muffin crumb. There are two different layers of cinnamon streusel, one inside the muffins and one on top. The top layer has more butter and walnuts for some extra texture and crunch.

CINNAMON STREUSEL

⅓ cup [45 g] all-purpose flour

¼ cup [50 g] granulated sugar

¼ cup [50 g] firmly packed brown sugar

1 Tbsp ground cinnamon

1 Tbsp cold salted butter, cut into ¼-in [6-mm] pieces

½ cup [60 g] coarsely chopped raw walnuts

BATTER

1 cup [140 g] all-purpose flour

½ cup [100 g] granulated sugar

1½ tsp baking powder

½ tsp baking soda

1 tsp kosher salt

5 Tbsp [85 g] salted butter, at room temperature

1 egg, plus 1 egg yolk

¾ cup [180 ml] sour cream

1½ tsp vanilla extract

1) Preheat the oven to 350°F [180°C]. Line a 12-well standard or 6-well jumbo muffin pan with paper liners or coat thoroughly with nonstick cooking spray.

2) To make the streusel: In a small bowl, whisk together the flour, granulated sugar, brown sugar, and cinnamon. Transfer half of the sugar mixture to another small bowl, and then add the butter and walnuts to the mixture in one of the bowls. With your fingers, rub the butter into the sugar mixture until the mixture resembles coarse sand (the streusel with the butter and walnuts will go on top of the muffins). Set both bowls aside.

CONT'D

3) To make the batter: In a medium bowl, whisk together the flour, granulated sugar, baking powder, baking soda, and salt. In a large bowl, beat the butter, egg, and egg yolk with an electric handheld or stand mixer at medium speed until well combined, about 30 seconds. Slowly add the sour cream and vanilla to the egg mixture and continue mixing at medium speed until smooth, about another 30 seconds. Add the flour mixture to the egg mixture in three batches, beating for about 15 seconds after each addition and scraping the bowl frequently. After the last addition, continue to beat at medium speed until the mixture is light and fluffy, about 1 minute. If you want to use a handheld whisk instead of an electric mixer, put on some sweat bands and your favorite workout music; your shoulder is about to get a great workout.

4) Divide half of the batter equally among the prepared muffin wells and sprinkle each well with an equal amount of the plain streusel (without the nuts and butter). Divide the remaining batter equally among the wells and sprinkle each with an equal amount of the nuts-and-butter streusel.

5) Bake until the tops are golden brown and a muffin bounces back when you poke it gently in the center with a finger, 22 to 26 minutes for standard muffins or 30 to 35 minutes for jumbo.

6) Remove the muffins from the oven and let cool in the pan for 5 minutes. Carefully lift the muffins from the pan and transfer them to a wire rack to cool a little more. (Use a butter knife to lift the muffins out if you didn't use paper liners.) Serve warm.

MORNING GLORY
MUFFINS

MAKES 12 REGULAR OR 6 JUMBO MUFFINS

These savory-sweet glories are perfect for summertime, when gardens—maybe yours—and farmers' markets are overflowing with zucchini. Packed with that prolific vegetable and lots of carrots, these muffins get a little zing from orange zest and ginger, crunch from nuts and sunflower seeds (which are optional), and sweetness from dried fruit. What a delicious way to sneak more vegetables into your diet!

This recipe accommodates a variety of substitutions: you could try shredded jicama, parsnips, apples, and/or drained, crushed pineapple for some of the zucchini and carrot. If you don't care for currants, dried cherries, sultanas, or cranberries are good alternatives. Not into nuts? No problem, leave them out. For any variations you invent, just be sure to use the same amount of shredded fresh vegetables (or fruit) to ensure the balance of flavors and texture.

6 Tbsp [85 g] salted butter, melted and cooled

2 eggs

⅓ cup [80 ml] whole milk

1 tsp vanilla extract

2 tsp orange zest (about 1 orange)

⅔ cup [130 g] firmly packed brown sugar

1⅓ cups [180 g] all-purpose flour

1½ tsp baking powder

½ tsp kosher salt

1 tsp ground ginger

¼ tsp ground cinnamon

1½ cups [180 g] shredded zucchini

1½ cups [180 g] shredded carrots

⅔ cup [75 g] coarsely chopped pecans or walnuts, toasted (see page 15)

½ cup [80 g] dried currants or raisins

2 Tbsp sunflower seeds (optional)

1) Preheat the oven to 350°F [180°C]. Line a 12-well standard or 6-well jumbo muffin pan with paper liners or coat thoroughly with nonstick cooking spray.

2) In a large bowl, whisk together the melted butter and the eggs. Add the milk, vanilla, orange zest, and brown sugar and whisk until well combined. In a medium bowl, whisk together the flour, baking powder, salt, ginger, and cinnamon.

CONT'D

3) Add the zucchini, carrots, pecans, currants, and flour mixture to the butter mixture and use a rubber spatula to carefully fold together until just combined. Be careful not to overmix, or your muffins will be tough; the batter should still have a couple of streaks of flour. It may seem like the large amount of shredded veggies could prevent the muffins from holding together, but don't worry; the batter will puff up in the oven and you'll have beautiful, perfect muffins.

4) Divide the batter equally among the prepared muffin wells. (It's okay to mound this batter up to the top of the cups; it won't spill over.) Then sprinkle each filled well with an equal amount of sunflower seeds (if using).

5) Bake until the tops are golden brown and a muffin bounces back when you poke it gently in the center with a finger, 24 to 27 minutes for standard muffins or 34 to 37 minutes for jumbo.

6) Remove the muffins from the oven and let cool in the pan for 5 to 10 minutes. Carefully lift the muffins from the pan and transfer them to a wire rack to cool a little more. (Use a butter knife to lift the muffins out if you didn't use paper liners.) Serve warm.

Variation

Sweet Potato Muffins with Cranberries and Pecans: Substitute 3 cups [360 g] peeled, shredded sweet potato for the carrots and zucchini. Substitute ½ cup [70 g] dried cranberries (or 1 cup [110 g] fresh or frozen cranberries if you prefer their tart flavor) for the currants. Substitute ⅔ cup [75 g] coarsely chopped toasted pecans for the walnuts. Omit the sunflower seeds. Bake as directed.

BANANA, WALNUT, AND CHOCOLATE CHIP
MUFFINS

MAKES 12 REGULAR OR 6 JUMBO MUFFINS

Like many diehard fans of banana bread are known to do, I am so fond of these muffins that I purposely let bananas get overripe and mushy just to have an excuse to make them. I'll even buy bananas that way if I see those black-flecked beauties cast off in the corner of the banana display at the market; I see them as black gold. The slight tang from the sour cream in this recipe offsets the sweetness of the bananas and chocolate chips, but you can use low-fat or whole milk in place of the sour cream if you don't have any handy, and the muffins will still be delicious. I prefer to use semisweet chocolate chips or chunks, but you can substitute milk chocolate or bittersweet chips. If you somehow manage to have leftovers, three regular-sized muffins will make a spectacular Muffin Bread Pudding (page 94).

6 Tbsp [85 g] salted butter, melted and cooled

2 eggs

⅓ cup [80 g] sour cream

1 tsp vanilla extract

1⅓ cups [300 g] mashed overripe bananas

1⅓ cups [180 g] all-purpose flour

⅔ cup [130 g] sugar

1½ tsp baking powder

½ tsp kosher salt

1⅓ cups [145 g] coarsely chopped walnuts, toasted (see page 15)

1 cup [180 g] semisweet chocolate chips or chunks

1 recipe Basic Streusel (page 23)

1) Preheat the oven to 350°F [180°C]. Line a 12-well standard or 6-well jumbo muffin pan with paper liners or coat thoroughly with nonstick cooking spray.

2) In a large bowl, whisk together the melted butter and the eggs. Add the sour cream, vanilla, and bananas and whisk until well combined. In a medium bowl, whisk together the flour, sugar, baking powder, and salt.

3) Add the flour mixture to the banana mixture and use a rubber spatula to carefully fold together until just combined. Gently fold in the walnuts and chocolate chips. Be careful not to overmix, or your muffins will be tough; the batter should still have a couple of streaks of flour.

4) Divide the batter equally among the prepared muffin wells and mound each filled well with an equal amount of the streusel.

CONT'D

5) Bake until the tops are golden brown and a muffin bounces back when you poke it gently in the center with a finger, 22 to 26 minutes for standard muffins or 30 to 35 minutes for jumbo.

6) Remove the muffins from the oven and let cool in the pan for 5 to 10 minutes. Carefully lift the muffins from the pan and transfer them to a wire rack to cool a little more. (Use a butter knife to lift the muffins out if you didn't use paper liners.) Serve warm.

 *Variations*

Banana-Strawberry Muffins: Omit the walnuts and chocolate chips. Fold 1½ cups [210 g] fresh or frozen strawberries, cut into ½-in [12-mm] chunks, into the batter before spooning it into the muffin wells. Bake as directed.

Banana-Nutella Muffins: Omit the walnuts and chocolate chips. Divide half of the batter equally among the muffin cups, and top each with 1½ tsp Nutella (or 1 Tbsp Nutella for jumbo muffins). Divide the remaining batter equally among the wells. Bake as directed.

MEXICAN CHOCOLATE-ZUCCHINI
MUFFINS

MAKES 12 REGULAR OR 6 JUMBO MUFFINS

Zucchini grows well where I live in northern California . . . too well. Summer gardens featuring squash, tomatoes, herbs, and greens are popular in these parts, and every year around July my friends find themselves drowning in zucchini. I don't bother planting zucchini because everyone I know will be so desperate to unload their extras that I'll have all the fresh zucchini I can manage. Packing shredded zucchini into muffins is one of my favorite ways to use up this bounty. The batter is really thick, but don't be alarmed; the zucchini will release moisture while cooking, and the muffins will come out tender and moist. These muffins puff up with fantastic, almost impossible-looking domes and are a huge crowd-pleaser.

6 Tbsp [85 g] salted butter, melted and cooled

2 eggs

⅓ cup [80 ml] whole milk

2 tsp vanilla extract

2 tsp balsamic vinegar

¾ cup [150 g] firmly packed brown sugar

2 cups [230 g] shredded zucchini

1¾ cups [245 g] all-purpose flour

½ cup [40 g] unsweetened Dutch-process (alkalized) cocoa powder

¾ tsp baking powder

¾ tsp baking soda

1½ tsp kosher salt

1 tsp ground cinnamon

½ tsp chipotle chile powder

1 cup [180 g] semisweet chocolate chips

1) Preheat the oven to 350°F [180°C]. Line a 12-well standard or 6-well jumbo muffin pan with paper liners or coat thoroughly with nonstick cooking spray.

2) In a large bowl, whisk together the melted butter and the eggs. Add the milk, vanilla, balsamic vinegar, and brown sugar, and whisk until well combined. Then stir in the shredded zucchini. In a medium bowl, whisk together the flour, cocoa powder, baking powder, baking soda, salt, cinnamon, and chipotle chile powder.

CONT'D

3) Add the flour mixture to the zucchini mixture, toss in the chocolate chips, and use a rubber spatula to carefully fold together until just combined. Because the cocoa makes the batter so dark, it's a little harder to tell if you're overmixing with these muffins, so stop when you think you've just incorporated the dry ingredients.

4) Divide the batter equally among the prepared muffin wells (it's okay to fill them to the brim).

5) Bake until the tops are puffed and a muffin bounces back when you poke it gently in the center with a finger, 22 to 26 minutes for standard muffins or 30 to 35 minutes for jumbo.

6) Remove the muffins from the oven and let cool in the pan for 5 to 10 minutes. Carefully lift the muffins from the pan and transfer them to a wire rack to cool a little more. (Use a butter knife to lift the muffins out if you didn't use paper liners.) Serve warm.

CINNAMON-APPLE OATMEAL
MUFFINS

MAKES 12 REGULAR OR 6 JUMBO MUFFINS

These are wholesome and hearty, with chunks of fresh apple, a hint of cinnamon, and a crunchy oat topping. It's actually pretty tricky to nail oatmeal muffins; they are prone to being too dry or too gummy, and using oat flour (as opposed to cooked or raw oats in the batter) is one of the secrets to getting them to come out just right. If you can't find oat flour, you can make it at home by grinding old-fashioned rolled oats in a food processor or blender until they have the approximate texture of whole-wheat flour. One cup [100 g] of oats makes ¾ cup plus 1 Table-spoon [100 g] of oat flour. To make the oat flavor really pop, spread the oats in a single layer on a baking sheet and toast them in a preheated 375°F [190°C] oven until they are lightly browned, about 20 minutes, before grinding them into flour.

OAT TOPPING

½ cup [50 g] old-fashioned rolled oats (not instant or quick-cooking)

⅓ cup [45 g] all-purpose flour

6 Tbsp [90 g] firmly packed brown sugar

1 tsp ground cinnamon

4 Tbsp [55 g] salted butter, softened and cut into ½-in [12-mm] pieces

BATTER

1 egg

4 Tbsp [55 g] salted butter, melted and cooled slightly

½ cup [120 ml] whole milk

¼ cup [60 ml] sour cream

¾ cup [150 g] firmly packed brown sugar

½ tsp vanilla extract

1 apple, unpeeled, cut into ½-in [12-mm] pieces (Gala, Golden Delicious, and Honeycrisp are particularly good, but any kind of apple is fine)

¾ cup plus 1 Tbsp [100 g] oat flour

1 cup [140 g] all-purpose flour

¾ tsp baking powder

¼ tsp baking soda

1 tsp kosher salt

1) Preheat the oven to 375°F [190°C]. Line a 12-well standard or 6-well jumbo muffin pan with paper liners or coat thoroughly with nonstick cooking spray.

2) To make the topping: In a small bowl, stir together the rolled oats, all-purpose flour, brown sugar, and cinnamon. Using your fingers or a pastry cutter, rub or cut the butter into the flour mixture until it is chunky and only a few pea-size pieces of butter are visible.

3) To make the batter: In a large bowl, whisk together the egg and melted butter. Add the milk, sour cream, brown sugar, and vanilla and whisk until well combined. Then stir in the chopped apple. In another large bowl, whisk together the oat flour, all-purpose flour, baking powder, baking soda, and salt.

4) Add the flour mixture to the egg mixture and use a rubber spatula to carefully fold together until just combined. Be careful not to overmix, or your muffins will be tough; the batter should still have a couple of streaks of flour.

5) Divide the batter equally among the prepared muffin wells. Mound each filled well with an equal amount of oat topping.

6) Bake until the tops are puffed and a muffin bounces back when you poke it gently in the center with a finger, 18 to 24 minutes for standard muffins or 25 to 30 minutes for jumbo.

7) Remove the muffins from the oven and let cool in the pan for 5 minutes. Carefully lift the muffins from the pan and transfer them to a wire rack to cool a little more. (Use a butter knife to lift the muffins out if you didn't use paper liners.) Serve warm.

Variation

Cinnamon-Pear Oatmeal Muffins: Substitute 2 small ripe but firm unpeeled pears (Bosc, Bartlett, and Anjou are recommended) for the apple. Bake as directed.

PUMPKIN-SPICE MUFFINS
WITH PUMPKIN SEED TOPPING

MAKES 12 REGULAR OR 6 JUMBO MUFFINS

Perfect for taking advantage of the fall harvest, these moist pumpkin muffins are spiced with the familiar flavors of seasonal and holiday traditions, using the handy ingredients from your pie-making cupboard: cinnamon, nutmeg, ginger, and allspice. These muffins are a bit denser than our other muffins, and crunchy toasted pecans and *pepitas* add a bit of texture. Pair them with a cup of hot coffee for a great start on a chilly morning.

PUMPKIN SEED STREUSEL

2½ Tbsp cold salted butter, cut into ½-in [12-mm] pieces

⅓ cup [45 g] all-purpose flour

3½ Tbsp firmly packed brown sugar

¼ cup [35 g] raw unsalted pepitas (pumpkin seeds)

BATTER

6 Tbsp [85 g] salted butter, melted and cooled

2 eggs

3½ Tbsp whole milk

1 tsp vanilla extract

1½ cups [340 g] canned or fresh pumpkin purée or butternut squash purée

1⅓ cups [180 g] all-purpose flour

¾ cup [150 g] granulated sugar

1½ tsp baking powder

½ tsp kosher salt

2 tsp ground cinnamon

2 tsp ground ginger

½ tsp ground nutmeg

½ tsp ground allspice

1 cup [110 g] coarsely chopped pecans, toasted (see page 15)

1) Preheat the oven to 350°F [180°C]. Line a 12-well standard or 6-well jumbo muffin pan with paper liners or coat thoroughly with nonstick cooking spray.

2) To make the streusel: In the bowl of a food processor fitted with the metal blade, pulse the butter, flour, and brown sugar in 1-second intervals until the butter is cut into pea-size pieces. (Alternatively, combine the butter, flour, and brown sugar in a bowl and use two knives or rub between your fingers to break up the butter into pea-size pieces.) Stir in the pepitas. The streusel should be a mixture of crumbly and chunky. Set aside.

CONT'D

3) To make the batter: In a large bowl, whisk together the melted butter and the eggs. Add the milk, vanilla, and pumpkin purée and whisk until well combined. In a medium bowl, whisk together the flour, granulated sugar, baking powder, salt, cinnamon, ginger, nutmeg, and allspice.

4) Add the flour mixture to the pumpkin mixture and use a rubber spatula to carefully fold together until just combined. Gently fold in the pecans. Be careful not to overmix, or your muffins will be tough; the batter should still have a couple of streaks of flour.

5) Divide the batter equally among the prepared muffin wells and mound each filled well with an equal amount of streusel.

6) Bake until the tops are golden brown and a muffin bounces back when you poke it gently in the center with a finger, 22 to 26 minutes for standard muffins or 30 to 35 minutes for jumbo.

7) Remove the muffins from the oven and let cool in the pan for 5 to 10 minutes. Carefully lift the muffins from the pan and transfer them to a wire rack to cool a little more. (Use a butter knife to lift the muffins out if you didn't use paper liners.) Serve warm.

GINGERBREAD

MUFFINS

MAKES 12 REGULAR OR 6 JUMBO MUFFINS

Serve these spicy gingerbread muffins as part of a holiday brunch spread or bring them to the office and be the office hero. These muffins are light, not dense and sticky like traditional gingerbread. The crystallized ginger adds a bit of texture and a pleasant bite.

6 Tbsp [85 g] salted butter, melted and cooled

2 eggs

⅓ cup [80 ml] buttermilk

½ cup [120 ml] molasses

½ cup [100 g] firmly packed brown sugar

1 tsp vanilla extract

1⅓ cups [180 g] all-purpose flour

1 tsp baking powder

1 tsp baking soda

½ tsp kosher salt

1 tsp ground ginger

1 tsp ground cinnamon

½ tsp ground allspice

¼ tsp ground cloves

⅛ tsp freshly ground black pepper

3 Tbsp chopped crystallized ginger

1 tsp confectioners' sugar (optional)

1) Preheat the oven to 325°F [165°C]. Line a 12-well standard or 6-well jumbo muffin pan with paper liners or coat thoroughly with nonstick cooking spray.

2) In a large bowl, whisk together the melted butter and the eggs. Add the buttermilk, molasses, brown sugar, and vanilla and whisk until well combined. In another large bowl, whisk together the flour, baking powder, baking soda, salt, ground ginger, cinnamon, allspice, cloves, and black pepper. Stir in the chopped crystallized ginger.

3) Add the flour mixture to the butter mixture and use a rubber spatula to carefully fold together until just combined. Be careful not to overmix, or your muffins will be tough; the batter should still have a couple of streaks of flour.

4) Divide the batter equally among the prepared muffin wells. Because these muffins have a lot of moisture, they are prone to collapsing a bit in the center. To prevent this, do not fill the muffin wells more than two-thirds full (if you have a little extra batter, make it into pancakes, see page 93) and do not open the oven to rotate the pans during baking.

CONT'D

5) Bake until the tops are puffed and a muffin bounces back when you poke it gently in the center with a finger, 18 to 22 minutes for standard muffins or 25 to 28 minutes for jumbo. Because these muffins are dark in color, it's a little more difficult to tell when they're done. If you're not sure, then slip a small sharp knife or a metal skewer into the center of a muffin; if it comes out clean, then the muffins are done.

6) Remove the muffins from the oven and let cool in the pan for 5 to 10 minutes. Carefully lift the muffins from the pan and transfer them to a wire rack to cool a little more. (Use a butter knife to lift the muffins out if you didn't use paper liners.)

7) Dust the tops with confectioners' sugar just before serving, if desired. Serve warm.

MEYER LEMON-POPPY SEED MUFFINS
WITH LEMON GLAZE

MAKES 12 REGULAR OR 6 JUMBO MUFFINS

When winter rolls around, I get excited. Not for the holidays or snow . . . but for Meyer lemons. I go lemon crazy, making lemon pies, lemon grilled fish, lemon cocktails, and these gorgeous Meyer lemon muffins. You can use regular Eureka lemons and make delightful muffins, but try Meyers if you can get them; they'll add a heady floral note and just a tiny touch of sweetness. I also highly recommend using chia seeds for the traditional poppy seeds if you can get them. I've included a variation using chia, and everyone who has tried it has loved them.

2 Meyer lemons (about ½ lb [230 g])

6 Tbsp [85 g] salted butter, melted and cooled

2 eggs

⅓ cup [80 ml] sour cream

1 tsp vanilla extract

1⅓ cups [180 g] all-purpose flour

¾ cup [150 g] granulated sugar

¾ tsp baking powder

½ tsp baking soda

½ tsp kosher salt

⅓ cup [45 g] poppy seeds, plus 1 tsp

½ cup [60 g] confectioners' sugar, plus up to 3 Tbsp more

1) Preheat the oven to 350°F [180°C]. Line a 12-well standard or 6-well jumbo muffin pan with paper liners or coat thoroughly with nonstick cooking spray.

2) Remove the zest from the lemons with a fine grater, carefully avoiding the bitter white pith, and place the zest in a large bowl. Juice the lemons, then put 2 Tbsp lemon juice in a medium bowl and add the remaining juice to the bowl with the lemon zest. Add the melted butter and the eggs to the bowl with the zest and whisk together. Add the sour cream and vanilla to the zest mixture and whisk until well combined. In a medium bowl, whisk together the flour, granulated sugar, baking powder, baking soda, salt, and ⅓ cup [45 g] poppy seeds.

3) Add the flour mixture to the butter mixture and use a rubber spatula to carefully fold together until just combined. Be careful not to overmix, or your muffins will be tough; the batter should still have a couple of streaks of flour.

CONT'D

4) Divide the batter equally among the prepared muffin wells.

5) Bake until the tops are golden brown and a muffin bounces back when you poke it gently in the center with a finger, 20 to 22 minutes for standard size or 25 to 28 minutes for jumbo.

6) While the muffins are baking, prepare a glaze by whisking the confectioners' sugar into the reserved lemon juice until smooth. The glaze should be quite thick, so that if you lift the whisk from the bowl it will run slowly off the end of the whisk in a thick, slow ribbon. If necessary, whisk in additional confectioners' sugar 1 Tbsp at a time.

7) Remove the muffins from the oven and let cool in the pan for 5 to 10 minutes. Carefully lift the muffins from the pan and transfer them to a wire rack to cool to room temperature, at least another 10 minutes. (Use a butter knife to lift the muffins out of the pan if you didn't use paper liners.)

8) Spoon some glaze evenly over each muffin (you may need to gently spread it over the tops of the muffins with the back of a dinner spoon, and it may run down the sides a bit), and then sprinkle the remaining 1 tsp poppy seeds evenly over the glazed muffins for decoration. Allow the glaze to set for 5 minutes. Serve immediately.

 *Variation*

Lemon Chia Muffins: Substitute ⅓ cup [60 g] chia seeds for the poppy seeds in Step 2. Bake as directed.

PEANUT BUTTER AND JELLY
MUFFINS

MAKES 12 REGULAR MUFFINS

Nikki, one of our cooks at The American, was inspired to create these PB&J muffins to use up the jam we make from our leftover fruit. A good thing, too, because now we get special requests to make these muffins all the time, often for clients who serve them at their business meetings. We like to imagine the look on a businessman's face as he bites into what he thinks is a boring bakery muffin when his mouth is flooded with a warm ribbon of peanut butter and strawberry jam. Does he smile? Laugh? Does the peanut butter stick to the roof of his mouth? We'll never know, but we suspect those high-powered business deals go down just a little easier because of these muffins, and we believe the business of breakfast at home will, too.

PEANUT STREUSEL

2½ Tbsp cold salted butter, cut into ½-in [12-mm] pieces

⅓ cup [45 g] all-purpose flour

3½ Tbsp firmly packed brown sugar

¼ cup [30 g] coarsely chopped dry-roasted unsalted peanuts

BATTER

6 Tbsp salted butter, melted and cooled

2 eggs

⅓ cup [80 ml] whole milk

1 tsp vanilla extract

1⅓ cups [180 g] all-purpose flour

¾ cup [150 g] granulated sugar

1½ tsp baking powder

½ tsp kosher salt

⅔ cup [170 g] peanut butter, crunchy or smooth

¾ cup [170 g] jam, jelly, or marmalade

1) Preheat the oven to 350°F [180°C]. Line a 12-well standard muffin pan with paper liners or coat thoroughly with nonstick cooking spray. (If you'd like to make jumbo muffins, see the following Note.)

2) To make the streusel: In the bowl of a food processor fitted with the metal blade, pulse the butter, flour, and brown sugar in 1-second intervals until the butter is cut into pea-size pieces. (Alternatively, combine the butter, flour, and brown sugar in a bowl and use two knives or rub between your fingers to break up the butter into pea-size pieces.) Stir in the chopped peanuts. The streusel should be a mixture of crumbly and chunky. Set aside.

CONT'D

3) To make the batter: In a large bowl, whisk together the melted butter and the eggs. Add the milk and vanilla and whisk until well combined. In a medium bowl, whisk together the flour, granulated sugar, baking powder, and salt.

4) Add the flour mixture to the butter mixture and use a rubber spatula to carefully fold together until just combined. Be careful not to overmix, or your muffins will be tough; the batter should still have a couple of streaks of flour.

5) Divide half of the batter equally among the prepared muffin wells. Spoon 1 tsp peanut butter and 1½ tsp jam into the center of each muffin. Divide the remaining batter equally among the wells, then top each filled well with another 1 tsp peanut butter and 1½ tsp jam. Mound the streusel evenly over the jam.

6) Bake until the tops are golden brown and a muffin bounces back when you poke it gently in the center with a finger, 20 to 22 minutes.

7) Remove the muffins from the oven and let cool for 5 to 10 minutes. Carefully lift the muffins from the pan and transfer them to a wire rack to cool a little more. (Use a butter knife to lift the muffins out if you didn't use paper liners.) Serve warm.

NOTE: To make jumbo PB&J muffins, assemble as directed using a 6-well jumbo muffin pan, but double the amount of peanut butter and jelly for each filling layer. Bake for 25 to 30 minutes and proceed as directed.

WHOLE-WHEAT BANANA MILLET
MUFFINS

MAKES 12 REGULAR OR 6 JUMBO MUFFINS

I was in high school when I encountered my first millet muffin at a café in my hometown, Laguna Beach, California. I'd never heard of millet and was fascinated by the crunchy yellow seeds in the sweet fluffy muffin, so I bought one every chance I got. Many years later, when I decided to develop my own version of millet muffins, I turned to several of my favorite baking ingredients—ripe mashed bananas, sour cream, and brown sugar—for inspiration.

CINNAMON-WALNUT STREUSEL

2½ Tbsp cold salted butter, cut into ½-in [12-mm] pieces

⅓ cup [45 g] all-purpose flour

3½ Tbsp firmly packed brown sugar

½ tsp ground cinnamon

⅔ cup [80 g] coarsely chopped raw walnuts

BATTER

6 Tbsp [85 g] salted butter, melted and cooled

2 eggs

⅓ cup [80 ml] sour cream

1 tsp vanilla extract

2 Tbsp dark rum

1 cup [230 g] mashed overripe bananas

⅔ cup [130 g] firmly packed brown sugar

¾ cup [105 g] all-purpose flour

¾ cup [105 g] whole wheat flour

1 tsp baking soda

½ tsp kosher salt

½ cup [105 g] millet seeds, rinsed and drained

1) Preheat the oven to 350°F [180°C]. Line a 12-well standard or 6-well jumbo muffin pan with paper liners or coat thoroughly with nonstick cooking spray.

2) To make the streusel: In the bowl of a food processor fitted with the metal blade, pulse the butter, flour, brown sugar, and cinnamon in 1-second intervals until the butter is cut into pea-size pieces.

CONT'D

(Alternatively, combine the butter, flour, and brown sugar in a bowl and use two knives or rub between your fingers to break up the butter into pea-size pieces.) Stir in the chopped walnuts. The streusel should be a mixture of crumbly and chunky. Set aside.

3) To make the batter: In a blender or in the bowl of a food processor fitted with the metal blade, blend the butter, eggs, sour cream, vanilla, rum, bananas, and brown sugar until smooth, about 30 seconds. (Alternatively, in a large bowl, mash the bananas thoroughly with a fork and then whisk in the other ingredients.) In a medium bowl, whisk together the flours, baking soda, salt, and millet.

4) Add the flour mixture to the banana mixture and use a rubber spatula to carefully fold together until just combined. Be careful not to overmix, or your muffins will be tough; the batter should still have a couple of streaks of flour.

5) Divide the batter equally among the prepared muffin wells and mound the streusel evenly over the batter.

6) Bake until the tops are golden brown and a muffin bounces back when you poke it gently in the center with a finger, 22 to 26 minutes for standard size or 30 to 35 minutes for jumbo.

7) Remove the muffins from the oven and let cool in the pan for 5 to 10 minutes. Carefully lift the muffins from the pan and transfer them to a wire rack to cool a little more. (Use a butter knife to lift the muffins out if you didn't use paper liners.) Serve warm.

TARTE TATIN
MUFFINS

MAKES 12 REGULAR OR 6 JUMBO MUFFINS

These upside-down caramel-apple muffins are sweet enough to serve for dessert—just add a scoop of vanilla bean ice cream for muffin à la mode—but I like to serve them as part of a decadent brunch. Caramelizing the apples on the stove top takes an extra 10 minutes and may seem like a lot of extra work, but if you get the apples started and then whip up the cinnamon muffin batter while they're cooking, then they really only take a few minutes more than the more basic muffins.

Do NOT use muffin liners with this recipe; you'll just get a sticky, papery mess. After you've removed the muffins, just soak the muffin pan in warm soapy water and the sticky caramel will come right off.

7 Tbsp [100 g] salted butter

¾ cup [150 g] sugar, plus ⅓ cup [65 g]

4 tart apples (such as Braeburn, Granny Smith, or Honeycrisp), each peeled, cored, and cut into 12 slices

1 egg

¼ cup [60 ml] whole milk

½ tsp vanilla extract

¾ cup [105 g] all-purpose flour

¾ tsp baking powder

¼ tsp kosher salt

¼ tsp ground cinnamon

1) Preheat the oven to 350°F [180°C]. Coat a 12-well standard or 6-well jumbo muffin pan thoroughly with melted butter or nonstick cooking spray.

2) In a 12- to 14-in [30- to 35-cm] nonstick skillet over medium heat, melt 4 Tbsp of the butter. Sprinkle ¾ cup [150 g] of the sugar evenly over the butter, and then add the apple slices, placing them flat-side down, on top of the sugar. (Don't worry if the apples don't all fit neatly into the pan, just crowd them all in. The apples will shrink and the caramel will bubble up over the apples to cook them.) Cook, occasionally shaking the pan gently to evenly distribute the caramel, until the sugar is beginning to brown, about 5 minutes. Using a spatula or tongs, carefully flip over the apple slices and continue cooking until they are beginning to brown and the caramel is an even light amber color, about another 5 minutes. Remove the skillet from the heat. Carefully spoon 4 apple slices (8 slices for jumbo muffins) into each prepared muffin well and then spoon any remaining caramel evenly over the apple slices. With the back of a spoon, gently press the apple slices evenly into the bottom of the wells. Set aside.

CONT'D

3) In a medium bowl, melt the remaining 3 Tbsp butter in the microwave and let cool slightly. Whisk the egg, milk, and vanilla into the melted butter until well combined. In a small bowl, whisk together the flour, remaining ⅓ cup [65 g] sugar, baking powder, salt, and cinnamon.

4) Add the flour mixture to the butter mixture and use a rubber spatula to carefully fold together until just combined. Be careful not to overmix, or your muffins will be tough; the batter should still have a couple of streaks of flour.

5) Spoon the batter over the apple slices, dividing it equally among the muffin wells. Smooth the tops with the back of a metal spoon or with your fingers dipped in cold water.

6) Bake until the tops are golden brown and a muffin bounces back when you poke it gently in the center with a finger, about 20 minutes for standard size or 30 minutes for jumbo.

7) Remove the muffins from the oven, place a clean, dry cutting board that is at least as large as the muffin pan facedown on the pan and then, using pot holders or two towels to hold them tightly together, carefully flip the cutting board and muffin pan over so that the muffin pan is facedown on top of the cutting board. Let cool in the pan for 5 minutes and then carefully lift the muffin pan off the muffins. (If a few apple slices stick in the muffin wells, just scoop them out with a spoon and tuck them back into place on the muffins.) Serve warm.

SPELT *AND* PEARL BARLEY
MUFFINS

MAKES 12 REGULAR OR 6 JUMBO MUFFINS

Hearty and satisfying, moist and pleasantly chewy, these whole-grain muffins are a nutritional winner. Pearl, or pearled, barley has been polished to remove the bran. Pearl barley cooks faster and is softer than hulled barley. Spelt is an ancient strain of wheat that originated over eight thousand years ago in the Middle East. Higher in protein and sweeter than our modern wheat, it has a nutty flavor and works well as a substitute for whole wheat in any recipe. Don't discard the barley cooking water; it's delicious and packed with vitamins. Strain the cooked barley over a bowl to catch the water, then stir in 1 teaspoon of maple syrup and pour over ice for a tasty and nutritious thirst quencher.

½ cup [100 g] pearl barley

1½ cups [360 ml] water

1½ cups [210 g] whole-grain spelt flour (or white whole-wheat flour)

3 Tbsp [20 g] ground flaxseeds (optional)

2 tsp baking powder

½ tsp baking soda

1 tsp kosher salt

2 eggs

2 Tbsp vegetable oil

2 Tbsp pure maple syrup

1 cup [240 ml] buttermilk

1 cup [80 g] shredded Gruyère or Comté cheese

2 tsp minced fresh thyme or 1 tsp dried thyme

2 tsp minced fresh sage or 1 tsp dried rubbed sage

1 Tbsp minced fresh parsley or 1½ tsp dried parsley

2 Tbsp toasted sesame seeds

1) In a small saucepan over medium heat, bring the barley and water to a boil. Cover the pan, turn the heat to low, and simmer until the barley is fully cooked (the grains will puff and burst slightly when done), 40 to 50 minutes. Remove from the heat, strain off any remaining cooking water, and allow the barley to cool while you prepare the other ingredients.

2) Preheat the oven to 400°F [200°C]. Line a 12-well standard or 6-well jumbo muffin pan with paper liners or coat thoroughly with nonstick cooking spray.

CONT'D

3) In a medium bowl, whisk together the spelt flour, ground flaxseeds (if using), baking powder, baking soda, and salt. In a large bowl, whisk together the eggs, vegetable oil, maple syrup, and buttermilk until well combined. Stir the cheese, herbs, and cooked barley into the egg mixture. Add the flour mixture to the egg mixture and use a rubber spatula to carefully fold together until just combined. Be careful not to overmix, or your muffins will be tough; the batter should still have a couple of streaks of flour.

4) Divide the batter among the prepared muffin wells and sprinkle the sesame seeds evenly over the filled wells.

5) Bake until the tops are golden brown and a muffin bounces back when you poke it gently in the center with a finger, 15 to 18 minutes for standard muffins or 20 to 24 minutes for jumbo.

6) Remove the muffins from the oven and let cool in the pan for 5 to 10 minutes. Carefully lift the muffins from the pan and transfer them to a wire rack to cool a little more. (Use a butter knife to lift the muffins out if you didn't use paper liners.) Serve warm (with a side of self-congratulation that you're serving something so healthful).

Variation

Spelt and Pearl Barley Fruit Muffins: Increase the pure maple syrup to ¼ cup [60 ml]. Decrease the buttermilk to ¾ cup [180 ml]. Omit the cheese and herbs. Add ½ tsp ground cinnamon with the baking powder in Step 3. Add one apple (Golden Delicious is recommended, but any will do), unpeeled, cored, and shredded, with the buttermilk in Step 3. Fold 1 cup [90 g] dried cherries, raisins, currants, or dried cranberries into the batter before spooning it into the muffin wells. Bake as directed.

WILD RICE AND SHIITAKE
MUFFINS

MAKES 12 REGULAR OR 6 JUMBO MUFFINS

Wild rice is actually not rice but the seed of a variety of long-grain marsh grasses that are native to North America and China. Prized for its unique nutty flavor and wonderful chewy texture, wild rice is often paired with earthy mushrooms in soups and stuffings. Here the two have been combined in a savory muffin that can accompany herb-roasted chicken or roast beef. You can cook the wild rice up to 2 days in advance; just store the cooked rice in the refrigerator until ready to use.

⅔ cup [120 g] wild rice (use 100% wild rice, not a blend), rinsed and drained

1½ cups [360 ml] water

½ cup [115 g] salted butter

1 medium yellow onion, cut into ¼-in [6-mm] pieces

8 oz [230 g] shiitake mushrooms, stemmed and cut into ½-in [12-mm] pieces

2 tsp minced fresh thyme or 1 tsp dried thyme

2 eggs

1 cup [140 g] all-purpose or white whole-wheat flour

4 tsp sugar

1 tsp baking powder

1½ tsp kosher salt

1) In a small saucepan over medium heat, bring the rice and water to a boil. Cover, turn the heat to low, and simmer until the rice is fully cooked (the grains will puff and burst slightly when done), 40 to 50 minutes. Remove from the heat, strain off any remaining cooking water, and allow the rice to cool while you prepare the other ingredients.

2) In a medium skillet over medium heat, melt 2 Tbsp [30 g] of the butter. Add the onions and shiitakes and cook, stirring occasionally, until the onions are translucent and just beginning to brown around the edges and the mushrooms are cooked through, about 8 minutes. Turn off the heat, and then add the thyme and stir to combine. Set aside.

3) Preheat the oven to 425°F [220°C]. Line a 12-well standard or 6-well jumbo muffin pan with paper liners or coat thoroughly with nonstick cooking spray.

CONT'D

4) In a large bowl, melt the remaining 6 Tbsp [85 g] butter in the microwave. Let cool slightly. Whisk the eggs into the melted butter and then stir in the rice-mushroom mixture. In a medium bowl, whisk together the flour, sugar, baking powder, and salt. Add the flour mixture to the egg mixture and use a rubber spatula to carefully fold together until just combined. Be careful not to overmix, or your muffins will be tough; the batter should still have a couple of streaks of flour.

5) Divide the batter equally among the prepared muffin wells.

6) Bake until the tops are golden brown and a muffin bounces back when you poke it gently in the center with a finger, 15 to 18 minutes for standard muffins or 20 to 24 minutes for jumbo.

7) Remove the muffins from the oven and let cool in the pan for 5 to 10 minutes. Carefully lift the muffins from the pan and transfer them to a wire rack to cool a little more. (Use a butter knife to lift the muffins out if you didn't use paper liners.) Serve warm.

QUINOA MUFFINS
WITH CHEDDAR, APPLES, AND ROSEMARY

MAKES 12 REGULAR OR 6 JUMBO MUFFINS

These muffins may actually be my lasting contri-bution to mankind. I love them that much. They're savory muffins, but the apples and brown sugar pull them back slightly toward the sweet side. The Ched-dar cheese and quinoa crisp up on top of the muffin, offering an unexpected bit of crunch. Red, white, and black quinoa all work equally well in this recipe, but I think that red quinoa makes the prettiest ver-sion. I like to serve these with any kind of pork roast or chops.

½ cup [90 g] red quinoa, rinsed and drained

1 cup [240 ml] water

4 Tbsp [55 g] salted butter, melted and cooled slightly

2 eggs

⅔ cup [160 ml] buttermilk

⅓ cup [65 g] firmly packed brown sugar

1 Granny Smith or other very tart apple, unpeeled, cored and shredded

1 cup [80 g] shredded Cheddar cheese

1½ cups [210 g] all-purpose flour

1 tsp baking powder

1 tsp baking soda

1 tsp kosher salt

2 tsp minced fresh rosemary or 1 tsp dried rosemary

1) In a small saucepan over medium heat, bring the quinoa and water to a boil. Stir, turn the heat to low, and simmer, covered, until the quinoa is fully cooked (the germ will spiral out of the grain when done), 15 to 20 minutes. Remove from the heat, strain off any remaining cooking water, and allow the quinoa to cool while you prepare the other ingredients.

2) Preheat the oven to 350°F [180°C]. Line a 12-well standard or 6-well jumbo muffin pan with paper liners or coat thoroughly with nonstick cooking spray.

3) In a large bowl, whisk together the butter, eggs, buttermilk, and brown sugar, and then stir in the quinoa, shredded apple, and shredded Cheddar. In a medium bowl, whisk together the flour, baking pow-der, baking soda, salt, and rosemary. Add the flour mixture to the egg mixture and use a rubber spatula to carefully fold together until just combined. The batter will be quite thick. Be careful not to overmix, or your muffins will be tough; the batter should still have a couple of streaks of flour.

4) Divide the batter among the prepared muffin wells. It's okay to mound up the batter to the top of the wells for these muffins.

CONT'D

5) Bake until the tops are golden brown and a muffin bounces back when you poke it gently in the center with a finger, 20 to 24 minutes for standard muffins or 26 to 30 minutes for jumbo.

6) Remove the muffins from the oven and let cool in the pan for 5 minutes. Carefully lift the muffins from the pan and transfer them to a wire rack to cool a little more. (Use a butter knife to lift the muffins out if you didn't use paper liners.) Serve warm.

OLIVE OIL, CHÈVRE, AND PINE NUT

MUFFINS

MAKES 12 REGULAR OR 6 JUMBO MUFFINS

I got my inspiration for these muffins from a dish called *farinata*, which originated in Italy. It's a savory chickpea-flour flatbread that's topped with anything from grilled onions to rosemary or cheese and served as a snack. Use the highest-quality olive oil for the best flavor and eat these muffins within minutes of their leaving the oven, or warm them before serving so that the chèvre is melted and warm.

½ cup [60 g] chickpea flour

¾ cup [180 ml] buttermilk

¾ cup [90 g] pine nuts, toasted (see page 15)

2 eggs

⅔ cup [160 ml] extra-virgin olive oil

3 Tbsp honey

1⅓ cups [180 g] all-purpose flour

1½ tsp baking powder

½ tsp baking soda

1½ tsp kosher salt

1 Tbsp minced fresh rosemary or 1½ tsp dried rosemary

7 oz [200 g] fresh chèvre (goat cheese), crumbled and kept cold

1) In a large bowl, whisk together the chickpea flour and buttermilk until well blended and let sit at room temperature for 30 minutes to hydrate the flour.

2) Preheat the oven to 400°F [200°C]. Line a 12-well standard or 6-well jumbo muffin pan with paper liners or coat thoroughly with nonstick cooking spray.

3) Set aside 2 Tbsp of the pine nuts in a small bowl (for sprinkling on top) and coarsely chop the remaining pine nuts. Whisk the eggs, olive oil, and honey into the chickpea flour mixture until well combined. In a medium bowl, whisk together the all-purpose flour, baking powder, baking soda, salt, rosemary, and chopped pine nuts.

4) Add the flour mixture to the egg mixture, and then sprinkle in the crumbled goat cheese as you carefully fold together the ingredients until just combined. Be careful not to overmix, or your muffins will be tough; the batter should still have a couple of streaks of flour.

CONT'D

5) Divide the batter among the prepared muffin wells. Sprinkle the reserved pine nuts evenly over the filled wells.

6) Bake until the tops are puffed and a muffin bounces back when you poke it gently in the center with a finger, 15 to 17 minutes for standard muffins or 20 to 24 minutes for jumbo. Be careful not to over-bake these muffins, or they will be dry.

7) Remove the muffins from the oven and let cool in the pan for 5 minutes. Carefully lift the muffins from the pan and serve immediately. (Use a butter knife to lift the muffins out if you didn't use paper liners.) Serve warm.

FRESH CORN AND MASA MUFFINS WITH BACON AND JALAPEÑOS

MAKES 12 REGULAR OR 6 JUMBO MUFFINS

Masa harina is corn flour that's been soaked in lime and water, then rinsed and dried. This process is what gives tortillas, *sopes*, and tamales their distinctive flavor and soft texture, and those same qualities shine through in these muffins. Masa is also sometimes used to thicken chili, and that's exactly what I like to serve these muffins alongside, in place of the traditional corn bread.

1 tsp vegetable oil

1 small yellow onion, cut into ¼-in [6-mm] pieces

1½ cups [240 g] fresh corn kernels (or drained canned or frozen sweet corn kernels)

1 tsp minced fresh thyme or ½ tsp dried thyme

½ tsp freshly ground black pepper

1 cup [140 g] all-purpose flour

¼ cup [40 g] masa harina

2 Tbsp sugar

2½ tsp baking powder

¼ tsp baking soda

1 tsp kosher salt

6 Tbsp [85 g] salted butter, melted and cooled slightly

1 egg, plus 1 egg yolk

1 cup [240 ml] buttermilk

10 slices thick-cut bacon, cooked until crisp and then cut into ½-in [12-mm] pieces

2 jalapeños, stems and seeds removed and cut into ¼-in [6-mm] pieces (substitute 1 fresh Pasilla or Anaheim chile for less heat)

1 cup [80 g] shredded Cheddar or pepper Jack cheese

1) In a medium saucepan over medium heat, warm the vegetable oil until shimmering but not smoking. Add the onion and cook, stirring occasionally, until translucent, about 6 minutes. Add the corn, thyme, and black pepper and cook, stirring occasionally, for 1 minute more. Remove from the heat and let cool while you prepare the muffin batter.

2) Preheat the oven to 400°F [200°C]. Liberally butter a 12-well standard or 6-well jumbo nonstick muffin pan or coat thoroughly with nonstick cooking spray. Do not use muffin liners; the muffins will stick to the liners instead of forming a nice crunchy brown crust.

CONT'D

3) In a large bowl, whisk together the flour, masa harina, sugar, baking powder, baking soda, and salt. In a medium bowl, whisk together the butter, egg, egg yolk, and buttermilk. Add the buttermilk mixture, corn mixture, bacon, jalapeños, and cheese to the flour mixture and use a wooden spoon or rubber spatula to gently fold together until just combined. Be careful not to overmix, or your muffins will be tough.

4) Divide the batter equally among the prepared muffin wells.

5) Bake until the tops are puffed and a muffin bounces back when you poke it gently in the center with a finger, 18 to 20 minutes for standard muffins or 25 to 30 minutes for jumbo.

6) Remove the muffins from the oven, run a dinner knife around the edges to loosen any stuck muffins, and let cool in the pan for 5 to 10 minutes. Carefully remove the muffins from the pan, lifting with the dinner knife if needed, and transfer them to a wire rack to cool a little more. Serve warm.

CIDER-CORN BREAD
MUFFINS

MAKES 12 REGULAR OR 6 JUMBO MUFFINS

The hard (alcoholic) apple cider in these muffins serves two purposes: it lightens the batter, creating fluffy and airy muffins with a nice soft crumb, and it adds a fruity flavor that brings out the sweetness of the corn. Use a dry (unsweetened), carbonated, hard apple cider like Woodchuck, Wandering Aengus, or Steampunk. Look for whole-grain stone-ground cornmeal instead of the more common de-germed cornmeal; the flavor is much better. Serve these muffins warm from the oven as a side dish for dinner or for breakfast with plenty of Honey Butter (page 152) to slather on top.

⅔ cup [90 g] finely ground, stone-ground cornmeal

½ cup [120 ml] sour cream

½ cup [120 ml] hard apple cider

4 Tbsp [55 g] salted butter, melted and cooled

1 egg

2 Tbsp honey

2 Tbsp sugar

Fresh raw corn kernels cut from 1 cob of corn or ¾ cup [90 g] frozen sweet corn kernels

1⅛ cups [160 g] all-purpose flour

¾ tsp baking powder

½ tsp baking soda

1 tsp kosher salt

1) Preheat the oven to 400°F [200°C]. Coat a 12-well standard or 6-well jumbo muffin pan with nonstick spray. (I recommend not using muffin liners; these muffins will stick to the liners instead of developing a nice crunchy crust.)

2) In a large bowl, whisk together the cornmeal, sour cream, and cider. Let sit for 10 minutes to allow the cornmeal to soften, then whisk in the melted butter, egg, honey, and sugar. Stir in the corn kernels. In a medium bowl, whisk together the flour, baking powder, baking soda, and salt. Add the flour mixture to the cornmeal mixture and use a rubber spatula to gently fold together until just barely combined.

3) Divide the batter equally among the prepared muffin wells.

4) Bake until the tops are just beginning to brown and a muffin bounces back when you poke it gently in the center with a finger, about 15 minutes for standard muffins or about 20 minutes for jumbo.

5) Remove the pan from the oven and run a butter knife around the edges of the muffins to loosen. Let cool in the pan for 5 minutes and then remove carefully, using a butter knife to lift the muffins if needed, and transfer them to a wire rack to cool a little more. Serve warm.

PUMPERNICKEL
MUFFINS

MAKES 8 REGULAR OR 4 JUMBO MUFFINS

I love everything about these pumpernickel muffins: the nutty whole-grain flours, the unusual dark color, the chocolate and molasses, the contrasting caraway seed. Make the batter the night before you want to serve them and divide it equally among the muffin wells. Cover the pan and refrigerate until the next day. Put the pan straight from the refrigerator into the oven—then turn the oven on. The muffins will rise while the oven heats up. Serve them with Molasses Butter (page 152) or cream cheese.

1 egg

1½ Tbsp firmly packed brown sugar

3 Tbsp vegetable oil

2 Tbsp dark molasses

⅔ cup [160 ml] warm (but not hot) strong coffee

½ cup [70 g] all-purpose flour

½ cup [70 g] dark rye flour

½ cup [70 g] whole-wheat flour

4 tsp unsweetened Dutch-process (alkalized) cocoa powder

1 Tbsp active dry (not instant) yeast

1½ tsp kosher salt

2 tsp caraway seeds

⅓ cup [45 g] golden raisins

⅓ cup [40 g] coarsely chopped walnuts, toasted (see page 15)

1) Line 8 wells in a 12-well standard or 4 wells in a 6-well jumbo muffin pan with paper liners or coat thoroughly with nonstick cooking spray.

2) In a medium bowl, whisk together the egg, brown sugar, vegetable oil, and molasses. Whisking continuously, slowly add the warm coffee. In the bowl of a stand mixer fitted with the paddle attachment, mix the all-purpose flour, rye flour, whole-wheat flour, cocoa powder, yeast, salt, and caraway seeds on low speed just until combined, about 20 seconds. (Alternatively, whisk together in a large bowl.)

3) With the mixer still on low speed, slowly add the coffee mixture to the flour mixture. Turn the speed to medium-low and beat for 5 minutes. The batter will be wet and sticky. You don't need to worry about overmixing these muffins; you want them to be more chewy than fluffy. Turn the speed to low, add the raisins and walnuts, and mix just until combined, about 10 seconds. (Alternatively, add the coffee mixture to the flour mixture in the large bowl and use a wooden spoon to beat the mixture until very smooth, about 5 minutes. Then stir in the raisins and walnuts.)

CONT'D

4) Divide the batter equally among the prepared muffin wells (they will be about half full), then wrap the muffin pan tightly with plastic and refrigerate for at least 8 hours, or up to 24 hours.

5) When ready to bake, remove the plastic wrap and put the muffins in the cold oven. Turn the oven temperature to 350°F [180°C] (the muffins will rise as the oven heats up).

6) Bake until the tops are puffed and a muffin bounces back when you poke it gently in the center with a finger, about 20 minutes for standard muffins or 30 minutes for jumbo.

7) Remove the muffins from the oven and let cool in the pan for 5 to 10 minutes. Carefully lift the muffins from the pan and transfer them to a wire rack to cool a little more. (Use a butter knife to lift the muffins out if you didn't use paper liners.) Serve warm.

HAM AND FONTINA BREAKFAST
HAND PIES

MAKES TWELVE 3-IN [7.5-CM] HAND PIES

Calling these "muffins" may be stretching the definition a bit, but they are baked in a muffin tin, so I couldn't resist including this recipe. Add whatever herbs, vegetables, or breakfast meats catch your fancy to the egg filling that lurks inside the crunchy whole-grain crust. The crust also works really well for quiches and single-crust potpies, and it's just the right size for one standard 9-inch [23-cm] pie. Whole-grain spelt flour has all the nutritional advantages of whole wheat but has a sweeter and milder flavor. Keep any extra in your freezer, as whole-grain flours will go rancid faster than white flours. Vodka is one of my favorite tricks for foolproof pie crust. It adds malleability to the dough for easier handling, but inhibits gluten from forming and adds no flavor; it's much harder to overwork your dough. I recommend substituting up to half of the water called for in traditional pie crust recipes with ice-cold vodka.

CRUST

1⅔ cups [195 g] whole-grain spelt flour (or whole-wheat pastry flour)

1½ tsp kosher salt

10 Tbsp [150 g] cold salted butter, cut into ½-in [12-mm] cubes and then frozen for 10 minutes

2 Tbsp sour cream, crème fraîche, or plain Greek yogurt

2 Tbsp cold vodka

3 Tbsp cold water

FILLING

2 tsp vegetable oil

1 large yellow onion, cut into ¼-in [6-mm] pieces

8 eggs, plus 1 egg white (optional)

⅓ cup [80 ml] heavy cream

1 tsp kosher salt

½ tsp freshly ground black pepper

1 Tbsp minced fresh thyme or 1½ tsp dried thyme, crumbled

6 oz [170 g] uncured ham, cut into ¼-in [6-mm] pieces

2 cups [160 g] shredded fontina cheese

1) To make the crust: In the bowl of a food processor fitted with the metal blade, mix the spelt flour and salt with two 1-second pulses. Cut in the frozen butter with three or four 2-second pulses until the butter is about the size of peas, and then transfer the mixture to a large bowl. In a small bowl, whisk together the sour cream, vodka, and water. Add the sour cream mixture to the flour mixture and use a rubber spatula to stir until the dough just comes together. (Alternatively, whisk together the flour and salt in a large bowl. Add the frozen butter and cut in with a pastry cutter or two knives. Then add the sour cream mixture as directed.) Scrape the dough out onto a

CONT'D

lightly floured cutting board or clean countertop and use your hands to form the dough into about a 6-in [15-cm] disk. Wrap tightly in plastic and refrigerate while you prepare the other ingredients. (The dough may be made up to 2 days in advance and refrigerated until ready to use.)

2) To make the filling: In a 10- to 12-in [25- to 30-cm] nonstick skillet over medium heat, add 1 tsp of the vegetable oil and swirl to coat the pan. Add the onions and sauté, stirring occasionally, until they are just beginning to brown, about 8 minutes. Meanwhile, in a medium bowl, whisk together the eggs, cream, salt, and pepper. Using a heatproof rubber spatula, transfer the cooked onions to a medium bowl. Turn the heat to low, add the remaining 1 tsp vegetable oil, and swirl to coat the pan. Add the egg mixture and cook until almost done but still slightly runny, gently lifting the curds and letting raw egg run underneath instead of stirring, about 2 minutes. You want the eggs very soft and barely cooked because they will be cooking further in the oven while the hand pies bake. Transfer the scrambled eggs to the bowl with the onions and gently fold in the thyme, ham, and cheese.

3) Preheat the oven to 425°F [220°C]. Coat a 12-well standard muffin pan with nonstick cooking spray.

4) Remove the pastry dough from the refrigerator and divide it into 12 equal pieces. Using your hands, roll each piece gently into a ball and then gently flatten each into a 2-in [5-cm] disk with the heel of your hand. Dust a cutting board or clean countertop with flour and then use a rolling pin to roll one piece of dough into a 7-in- [17-cm-] diameter disk, dusting with additional flour as needed to prevent sticking. The dough will be very thin. Place the disk on top of one muffin well and then gently tuck the dough into the well, pressing gently up the sides to line the well with dough, allowing the excess to lie flat outside the muffin well. Spoon about 5 Tbsp of egg filling into each lined muffin well, filling it up to the top. Close the dough over the filling, pinching the dough together decoratively to seal. Repeat with the remaining 11 balls of dough.

5) In a small bowl, whisk the egg white (if using) with 1 tsp cold water and then use a pastry brush to lightly coat the tops of all the hand pies with the egg wash. Try to avoid letting the wash run down into the sides of the muffin wells; this could cause the pastry to stick.

6) Bake until the pastry tops are golden brown, 18 to 22 minutes.

CONT'D

7) Remove the pies from the oven, run a dinner knife around the edges to loosen, and let cool in the pan for 5 minutes. Carefully remove the pies from the pan, using a dinner knife to help lift the pies if needed, and transfer them to a wire rack to cool for 5 minutes more before serving.

 *Variations*

Mushroom and Swiss Breakfast Hand Pies: Slice 6 oz [170 g] shiitake, cremini, or button mushrooms and sauté with the onions in Step 2. Substitute Swiss (Emmenthal) or Gruyère cheese for the fontina and omit the ham. Bake as directed.

Scallion, Bacon, and Cheddar Breakfast Hand Pies: Slice 10 scallions (green and white parts) and add to the eggs with the onions and cheese in Step 2. Substitute Cheddar cheese for the fontina. Omit the thyme. Substitute 6 thick-cut pieces of cooked bacon, chopped into ½-in [12-mm] pieces, for the ham. Bake as directed.

Florentine Breakfast Hand Pies: Add a pinch of ground nutmeg to the eggs with the salt and pepper in Step 2. Substitute ⅔ cup [80 g] crumbled feta and 1¼ cups [100 g] shredded Cheddar cheese for the fontina. Chop 2 cups [40 g] baby spinach and fold into the scrambled eggs with the onions and cheese in Step 2. Bake as directed.

PANCAKES *AND* WAFFLES

A couple of the morning prep cooks at one of our restaurants discovered that blueberry muffin batter makes fantastic pancakes when thinned with a bit of milk, and they started making them for their own staff breakfast. I caught wind of this and figured that they'd make great waffles, too.

To make one batch of muffin batter into pancakes or waffles, increase the milk in the muffin recipe by ½ cup [120 ml]. If you want to use half the batter to bake muffins first, just stir ¼ cup [60 ml] milk (whole, low-fat, or nonfat work equally well) into the remaining batter before using it for pancakes or waffles. The best muffin batters to use for making waffles or pancakes:

- Bake-Sale Berry Muffins (page 27)
- Balsamic Strawberry Muffins (page 29)
- Ginger-Peach Muffins (page 32)
- Cranberry-Orange Muffins (page 34)
- Piña Colada Muffins (page 39)
- Apricot-Almond Muffins (page 36)
- Banana, Walnut, and Chocolate Chip Muffins (page 47)
- Morning Glory Muffins (page 43)
- Pumpkin-Spice Muffins (page 55)
- Cinnamon-Apple Oatmeal Muffins (page 52)
- Gingerbread Muffins (page 57)
- Whole-Wheat Banana Millet Muffins (page 65)
- Cider–Corn Bread Muffins (page 86)

MUFFIN BREAD PUDDING

Bread pudding is a great way to use up leftover muffins. It's best if you assemble it the day before and let it sit overnight in the refrigerator before baking it the next morning if you wish to serve it as a decadent breakfast or brunch dish, or the next evening if you're serving it for dessert.

Here is a list of the muffins in this book that I think are particularly delicious in bread pudding. And be sure to try it with the Brown Sugar–Bourbon Sauce (page 160). You won't be sorry.

- Bake-Sale Berry Muffins (page 27)
- Balsamic Strawberry Muffins (page 29)
- Ginger-Peach Muffins (page 32)
- Cranberry-Orange Muffins (page 34)
- Piña Colada Muffins (page 39)
- Apricot-Almond Muffins (page 36)
- Banana, Walnut, and Chocolate Chip Muffins (page 47)
- Sour Cream–Coffee Cake Muffins (page 41)
- Mexican Chocolate–Zucchini Muffins (page 49)
- Pumpkin-Spice Muffins (page 55)
- Cinnamon-Apple Oatmeal Muffins (page 52)
- Meyer Lemon–Poppy Seed Muffins (page 59)
- Gingerbread Muffins (page 57)

MUFFIN BREAD PUDDING

SERVES 4 TO 6

3 standard-size leftover muffins, cut into 1-in [2.5-cm] cubes

3 eggs, plus 4 egg yolks

½ tsp kosher salt

¼ cup [50 g] sugar

1 tsp vanilla extract

1 cup [240 ml] whole milk

½ cup [120 ml] heavy cream

½ cup [120 ml] buttermilk, crème fraîche, or kefir

1 recipe Brown Sugar–Bourbon Sauce (page 160), or your favorite topping

1) Butter a 9-by-5-in [23-by-12-cm] loaf pan and place the muffin squares in the pan.

2) In the bowl of a stand mixer fitted with the whisk attachment, or in a large bowl using a handheld mixer, beat the eggs, egg yolks, and salt on medium speed until well blended, about 1 minute. Add the sugar, vanilla, milk, cream, and buttermilk and beat on medium speed until thoroughly blended, about 30 seconds more.

3) Pour the egg mixture into the prepared loaf pan, pressing gently with your hands to make sure all of the muffins are completely soaked with custard. Cover with aluminum foil and refrigerate for at least 1 hour or up to 2 days.

4) Preheat the oven to 325°F [165°C].

5) Place the loaf pan, still covered in foil, in a larger pan with sides that are at least slightly higher than half the height of the loaf pan. Place the pan, with the loaf pan inside, in the oven and then pour enough scalding hot water (the hottest water from your tap is fine) into the pan to come halfway up the sides of the loaf pan.

6) Bake for about 40 minutes, then rotate the pan, remove the foil, and bake until the custard is just set or an instant-read thermometer inserted into the center of the pudding registers 160°F [70°C], about another 10 minutes.

7) Remove the pudding from the oven and let cool for about 10 minutes. Serve warm, topped with the bourbon sauce.

 *Variations*

Berry-Cinnamon Bread Pudding: Scatter 1 cup [120 g] fresh or frozen blueberries, raspberries, or strawberries, stemmed and cut into ½-in [12-mm] pieces, over and between the muffins in Step 1. Whisk 1 tsp ground cinnamon into the sugar before adding in Step 2. Proceed as directed.

Rum Raisin Bread Pudding: In a small bowl, soak ⅓ cup [60 g] raisins in ¼ cup [60 ml] dark rum for 15 minutes. Strain the raisins from the rum (reserving the rum) and scatter them over and between the muffin pieces in Step 1. Stir the reserved rum into the custard with the vanilla in Step 2 and proceed as directed.

Stone Fruit–Cardamom Bread Pudding: Cut 1 ripe unpeeled peach or 2 ripe unpeeled plums into ½-in [12-mm] pieces and scatter the pieces over and between the muffins in Step 1. Whisk ½ tsp ground cardamom into the sugar before adding in Step 2. Proceed as directed.

YAHOO!

BISCUITS

PERFECTLY EASY
CREAM BISCUITS

MAKES TEN 2-IN [5-CM] BISCUITS

Light, fluffy, baking-powder biscuits are universally popular, from the kitchen table at home to formal restaurants. My husband, Nate, and I love them solo, sandwiched, or in composed dishes like Biscuit Strata (page 146). What makes this recipe special is that these biscuits are ridiculously fast and easy; there's no need to cut in butter or worry about over-working the dough.

The cream biscuit breakthrough came on an uncharacteristically slow morning at our restaurant when Nate decided he wanted to create a biscuit-and-egg special. After a bit of research, he mixed, patted, and cut his way to this recipe, using ingredients that were in the shop. I walked in to find him covered in flour from head to toe and holding a plate of some of the most delicious biscuits either of us had ever tasted. We hope you agree.

1¾ cups [245 g] all-purpose flour

2 tsp sugar

2½ tsp baking powder

1½ tsp kosher salt

1½ cups [360 ml] heavy cream

2 Tbsp unsalted butter, melted (optional)

1) Preheat the oven to 475°F [240°C]. Line a baking sheet with parchment paper or coat with nonstick cooking spray.

2) In a medium bowl, whisk together the flour, sugar, baking powder, and salt. Add the cream and use a wooden spoon or rubber spatula to stir, scraping the flour off the sides of the bowl as you go, just until the dough forms a ball, about 30 seconds.

3) Scrape the biscuit dough out onto a lightly floured cutting board or countertop. Dust your hands with flour and gather the dough into a ball. Knead the dough 8 times, folding it back onto itself and rotating the ball a quarter turn (90 degrees) each time. Working your way from the center out, pat the dough ball into a round about ¾ in [2 cm] thick, dusting with additional flour if the dough begins to stick to your hands or the board.

4) Using a biscuit cutter dipped in flour between each cut, cut the dough into 10 rounds or squares, gathering the dough scraps and patting out for more biscuits as needed. Do not twist the biscuit cutter while cutting; this prevents maximum rise by sealing the edges together. (If you don't have a biscuit cutter, dip a sharp knife in flour and divide the dough into 10 equal chunks. Don't worry too much about the shape; they will expand in the oven.)

CONT'D

5) Place the biscuits on the prepared baking sheet, spacing them about 1 in [2.5 cm] apart. (At this point, you can store the unbaked biscuits: cover the biscuits on the sheet tightly with plastic wrap and refrigerate for up to 24 hours.)

6) Bake until puffed and golden brown, rotating the baking sheet halfway through, about 12 minutes. If you like, you can brush the hot biscuits with the melted butter after removing them from the oven. This gives the biscuits a shiny top and a little extra richness.

7) Transfer the biscuits to a wire rack to cool for 5 minutes. If you are not serving the biscuits right away, wrap them tightly in plastic or place them in a resealable bag and store in the freezer for up to 1 month. To serve, place the biscuits on a baking sheet and warm in a preheated 400°F [200°C] oven for 5 minutes.

 *Variations*

Herby: Whisk 1 Tbsp dried (and crumbled, if the bits are larger, as with rosemary and sage) or 2 Tbsp minced fresh herbs per batch into the flour mixture before you add the cream in Step 2. We like a mix of equal parts rosemary, thyme, and sage, but you can also add parsley, chives, savory, dill, or basil to the mix.

Meaty: Toss about 1½ cups [255 g] diced or shredded cooked meat (ham, smoked turkey, pulled pork, and chopped prosciutto are delicious) per batch into the flour mixture before you add the cream in Step 2.

Cheesy: Toss about 6 oz [170 g] shredded cheese per batch into the flour mixture before you add the cream in Step 2. You can use a combination of cheeses, if you wish, but do not use chèvre or fresh mozzarella. If you want to use a strongly flavored cheese like blue cheese or Gruyère, use only 2 oz [60 g] of the strong cheese and 4 oz [115 g] of something milder, like mild Cheddar or Jack.

CATHEAD

BISCUITS

MAKES TWELVE 2½-IN [6-CM] BISCUITS

This is a quick-and-easy "cut-in" buttermilk biscuit. According to legend, they're supposed to be as big as a cat's head—hence the name. I make mine a more reasonable size and I use all butter instead of the traditional lard or shortening, because I like butter's richness and flavor. Dredging the dough in flour and brushing the tops with melted butter makes a wonderful crust, so resist the urge to dust off the extra flour when you're preparing them for the pan. If you can get that icon of Southern biscuit making, White Lily Flour, substitute 3 cups [360 g] of it for both the all-purpose and the cake flour.

1½ cups [210 g] all-purpose flour, plus ¼ cup [35 g]

1½ cups [180 g] cake flour

1 Tbsp baking powder

½ tsp baking soda

2 tsp kosher salt

¾ cup [165 g] cold unsalted butter, cut into ¼-in [6-mm] cubes, plus 4 Tbsp [55 g], melted

1¼ cups [300 ml] buttermilk

1) Preheat the oven to 400°F [200°C]. Butter a 9-in [23-cm] round cake pan or an 8-by-8-in [20-by-20-cm] metal or glass square baking pan.

2) In a large bowl, whisk together the 1½ cups [210 g] all-purpose flour, cake flour, baking powder, baking soda, and salt. Scatter the butter cubes over the flour mixture and toss gently with a wooden spoon or rubber spatula until evenly coated. Cut the butter into the flour with a pastry cutter or two knives until the mixture resembles coarse meal but chunks of butter are still visible. (Alternatively, in the bowl of a food processor fitted with the metal blade, cut the butter into the flour mixture with about three 1-second pulses.) Make a well in the center of the mixture, pour in the cold buttermilk, and use a wooden spoon or rubber spatula to stir just until the dough comes together, scraping down the sides of the bowl as needed. The dough should be shaggy and a little sticky.

3) Place the remaining ¼ cup [35 g] all-purpose flour in a shallow bowl. Coat your hands well with flour, then pull off 12 approximately egg-size chunks of dough, dredge them thoroughly in the flour, and gently place the chunks next to each other, just touching, in the prepared pan. Resist the urge to smooth and shape the dough. Leave it rough and shaggy so you end up with a nice craggy crust.

CONT'D

4) Use a pastry brush to lightly coat the tops of the biscuits with the remaining 4 Tbsp [55 g] melted butter. Pour any remaining butter over the tops of the biscuits.

5) Bake until puffed and golden brown, rotating the baking pan halfway through, 15 to 17 minutes.

6) Transfer the biscuits to a wire rack to cool for 5 minutes. If you are not serving the biscuits right away, wrap them tightly in plastic or place in a resealable bag and store in the freezer for up to 1 month. To serve, place the biscuits on a baking sheet and warm in a preheated 400°F [200°C] oven for 5 minutes.

ANGEL BISCUITS

MAKES TEN 2-IN [5-CM] BISCUITS

I've heard that light, fluffy Angel Biscuits used to be called Bride's Biscuits, because even a novice cook can't ruin them. I find the old-fashioned reference amusing, but there's a nugget of truth in it: Angel Biscuits are pretty hard to mess up; using the three types of leaveners called for in the recipe, you can't help but end up with tall, light-as-air biscuits. These unusual yeasted biscuits do require advance planning: the dough comes together in minutes, but the biscuits need to rest for the yeast to develop, at least 2 hours and preferably overnight.

½ cup [110 g] cold unsalted butter, cut into ¼-in [6-mm] cubes, plus 2 Tbsp, melted and cooled

2 cups [280 g] all-purpose flour

⅔ cup [80 g] cake flour

2 Tbsp sugar

1¼ tsp active dry yeast (not instant)

1 Tbsp baking powder

½ tsp baking soda

2 tsp kosher salt

1 cup plus 2 Tbsp [270 ml] buttermilk

1) Put the butter cubes in a small bowl, cover with plastic, and chill in the freezer for 10 minutes while you prepare the other ingredients. In a large bowl, whisk together the all-purpose flour, cake flour, sugar, yeast, baking powder, baking soda, and salt.

2) Remove the butter from the freezer and scatter the butter cubes over the flour mixture. Cut the butter into the flour with a pastry cutter or two knives until the mixture resembles a coarse meal but chunks of butter are still visible. (Alternatively, put the flour mixture and butter in the bowl of a food processor fitted with the metal blade and cut the butter into the flour mixture with about five 1-second pulses, and then return the mixture to the large bowl.) Make a well in the center of the mixture, pour in the cold buttermilk, and use a wooden spoon or rubber spatula to stir just until the dough comes together, scraping down the sides of the bowl as needed. The dough should be shaggy and a little sticky.

CONT'D

3) Turn the dough out onto a well-floured cutting board or countertop and knead gently with floured hands about 20 times, folding it back onto itself and rotating the ball one-quarter turn (90 degrees) each time, until the dough is fairly smooth. Return the dough to the mixing bowl, cover tightly with plastic wrap, and refrigerate for at least 2 hours or up to 2 days.

4) Preheat the oven to 400°F [200°C]. Line a baking sheet with parchment paper or coat with nonstick cooking spray.

5) Remove the bowl from the refrigerator and turn the dough out onto a lightly floured cutting board or countertop. With a rolling pin or with your hands, roll or pat the dough out into a ¾-in- [2-cm-] thick disk. Using a biscuit cutter dipped in flour after each cut, cut out as many biscuits as you can. Then gather the scraps, gently press them together, and reroll to cut out as many additional biscuits as possible. (Alternatively, using a sharp knife dipped in flour after each cut, cut the dough into ten 2-in [5-cm] squares.) Transfer the biscuits to the prepared baking sheet, placing them at least 1 in [2.5 cm] apart. Cover with a kitchen towel and let rest for 30 minutes at room temperature so the biscuits can rise and the dough relaxes; this will help the biscuits keep their shape while baking.

6) Brush the biscuits with the remaining 2 Tbsp melted butter. Bake until puffed and golden brown, rotating the baking sheet halfway through, about 12 minutes.

7) Transfer the biscuits to a wire rack to cool for 5 minutes. If you are not serving the biscuits right away, wrap them tightly in plastic or place them in a resealable bag and store in the freezer for up to 1 month. To serve, place the biscuits on a baking sheet and warm in a preheated 400°F [200°C] oven for 5 minutes.

ULTRA-FLAKY
BISCUITS

MAKES NINE 3-IN [7.5-CM] BISCUITS

This recipe produces a flaky biscuit with dozens of even layers that are crunchy on the outside and soft and delicious inside. Every time I make them, usually just for special occasions because they take a little extra work, I get *oohs* and *aahs* at the dinner table. I like to start them the day before I serve so that I don't have to worry about them while I'm putting together the rest of the meal. At any of the steps calling for 30-minute rests, you can let the dough rest for up to 24 hours and pick the project up again the next day. The egg adds a bit of richness and structure to the biscuits, but if you want a more crumbly, shortbread-like texture, then replace the egg with ¼ cup [60 ml] heavy whipping cream.

14 Tbsp [190 g] cold unsalted butter, cut into ½-in [12-mm] cubes

2¾ cups [385 g] all-purpose flour

2 Tbsp sugar

1 Tbsp baking powder

½ tsp baking soda

2 tsp kosher salt

1 egg

¾ cup [180 ml] buttermilk

1) In a large bowl, toss the butter with 1 Tbsp of the flour until evenly coated. Transfer the coated butter to a small bowl and place in the freezer for about 10 minutes while you prepare the other ingredients.

2) In the same large bowl, whisk together the remaining flour, sugar, baking powder, baking soda, and salt. In a small bowl, whisk together the egg and buttermilk.

3) Remove the butter from the freezer, add it to the flour mixture, and use a wooden spoon or rubber spatula to toss gently until the butter is evenly distributed. Cut the butter into the flour with a pastry cutter or two knives until marble-size chunks of butter are visible. (Alternatively, in the bowl of a food processor fitted with the metal blade, cut the butter into the flour mixture with about three 1-second pulses, and then return the mixture to the mixing bowl.)

4) Add the buttermilk mixture to the flour mixture and and toss gently with the wooden spoon or rubber spatula until the dough just starts to clump together. It will be shaggy and pretty dry, and you should still see chunks of butter. Right about now you're probably thinking that there must be a typo in the recipe. Don't worry; it's going to work out, I promise! Cover the bowl with plastic wrap and refrigerate for 30 minutes to allow the flour to fully hydrate.

CONT'D

5) Dust a large clean cutting board or countertop with flour (a Silpat-style baking mat works well for this). Remove the bowl of dough from the refrigerator and scrape out the dough, along with any dry floury bits sticking to the bowl, onto the board. Coat your hands with flour and pat the dough into a rectangle about ¾ in [2 cm] thick, with the long side approximately twice as long as the short side. Starting at one of the short ends, carefully fold the dough into thirds, like a business letter (a bench scraper is a handy tool for folding and for squaring off the edges). It's fine if the dough isn't holding together well and is breaking up; just pat it gently back into place and keep going. After turning the dough so that the short (open) end is facing you, use your hands to press the layers together gently and neaten the dough, restoring its rectangular shape. Then use a rolling pin to roll the dough into another ½-in- [12-mm-] thick rectangle and fold into thirds like the first time, and turn again. Repeat the rolling (into a ½-in- [12-mm-] thick rectangle), folding, and turning twice more (for 4 folds total), rolling the dough into a ¾-in- [2-cm-] thick square after the last fold. Wrap in plastic and return to the refrigerator for at least 30 minutes or up to 24 hours.

6) Preheat the oven to 400°F [200°C]. Line a baking sheet with parchment paper or coat with nonstick cooking spray.

7) Remove the dough from the refrigerator and, using a biscuit cutter dipped in flour between each cut and pressing straight down without twisting, cut out as many biscuits as possible. Gather the scraps, press them together gently, and reroll to cut as many additional biscuits as possible. The biscuits from this second set will not be as pretty as the first, but they'll be just as delicious! (Alternatively, to make square biscuits, trim about ½ in [12 mm] off the edges of the square and then, using a large sharp knife dipped in flour between each cut, cut the square into 9 equal pieces. I like to roll up the bits trimmed off the edges, pinch the ends together, and bake them as well.)

8) Place the biscuits on the prepared baking sheet, spacing them at least 1 in [2.5 cm] apart.

9) Bake until puffed and golden brown, rotating the baking sheet halfway through, 12 to 15 minutes.

10) Transfer the biscuits to a wire rack to cool for 5 minutes. If you are not serving the biscuits right away, wrap them tightly in plastic or place in a resealable bag and store in the freezer for up to 1 month. To serve, place the biscuits on a baking sheet and warm in a preheated 400°F [200°C] oven for 5 minutes.

COCONUT OIL-SWEET POTATO
BISCUITS

MAKES TEN 2½-IN [6-CM] BISCUITS

My mother, who is a great cook, is obsessed with the little purple Japanese sweet potatoes called *murasakis*. She rubs them in coconut oil before slow-roasting them and serves them with grilled fish and sesame cucumber salad. They are ideal for this recipe, but you'll get great results with any variety. The recipe happens to be vegan and dairy-free. If you prefer a more traditional biscuit flavor, however, you can substitute buttermilk for the almond milk and vinegar and use butter instead of coconut oil.

1¾ cups [245 g] all-purpose flour

2½ tsp baking powder

½ tsp baking soda

1½ tsp kosher salt

1 medium sweet potato (about 5 oz [140 g]), roasted in an oven or cooked in a microwave until very soft, then peeled, thoroughly mashed, and cooled

⅓ cup [80 ml] unsweetened almond or soy milk

1 Tbsp apple cider vinegar

1 Tbsp firmly packed brown sugar

⅓ cup [65 g] unrefined coconut oil, poured or scooped into a small bowl and chilled in the refrigerator until firm, then cut into ½-in [12-mm] pieces

1 Tbsp granulated sugar (optional)

1) Preheat the oven to 400°F [200°C]. Line a baking sheet with parchment paper or coat with nonstick cooking spray.

2) In a large bowl, whisk together the flour, baking powder, baking soda, and salt until well mixed. In a medium bowl, whisk together the mashed sweet potato, almond milk, apple cider vinegar, and brown sugar.

3) Using a pastry cutter or two knives, cut the coconut oil into the flour mixture until no coconut oil pieces larger than a pea remain. (Alternatively, in the bowl of a food processor fitted with the metal blade, cut the oil into the flour mixture with about five 1-second pulses.)

4) Add the sweet potato mixture to the flour mixture and use a wooden spoon or rubber spatula to stir until the dough just comes together. The dough will be crumbly; squeeze it together gently to form a ball. Turn the dough out onto a lightly floured cutting board or countertop and knead gently 5 or 6 times to form a smooth ball. Return the dough to the mixing bowl, cover with plastic wrap, and let the dough rest in the refrigerator for at least 30 minutes or up to 24 hours.

5) Turn the dough out onto a lightly floured cutting board or countertop. Working your way from the center out, gently pat with your hands or use a rolling pin to roll the dough ball into a round disk about ¾ in [2 cm] thick. Pressing straight down and without twisting, use a biscuit cutter dipped in flour to cut as many biscuits as you can from the disk. Gather the scraps, gently pat out again, and cut as many additional biscuits as possible.

6) Place the biscuits on an ungreased baking sheet, spacing them at least 1 in [2.5 cm] apart, and sprinkle them evenly with the granulated sugar, if desired.

7) Bake until puffed and golden on top, 12 to 15 minutes.

8) Transfer the biscuits to a wire rack to cool for 5 minutes. If you are not serving the biscuits right away, wrap them tightly in plastic or place them in a resealable bag and store in the freezer for up to 1 month. To serve, place the biscuits on a baking sheet and warm in a preheated 400°F [200°C] oven for 5 minutes.

 *Variations*

Orange-Coconut Sweet Potato Biscuits: Add 2 tsp orange zest to the coconut oil mixture in Step 3.

Ginger-Coconut Sweet Potato Biscuits: Whisk 1 tsp ground ginger into the flour mixture in Step 2 before cutting in the coconut oil and stir ⅓ cup [50 g] coarsely chopped crystallized ginger into the coconut oil mixture in Step 3 before adding it to the flour mixture.

HONEY-LAVENDER
BISCUITS

MAKES EIGHT 2-IN [5-CM] BISCUITS

Take a big whiff of these biscuits when they come out of the oven, and you'll get a noseful of earthy honey and floral lavender. Their texture is somewhere between that of a biscuit and a shortbread, and they're not as sweet as you might expect from their lovely aroma. Serve them at dinner with, say, a simple roasted chicken or pork loin and a fresh green salad, or dress them up for dessert by splitting them and topping them with fresh berries, a dollop of Raspberry Curd (page 156), and a scoop of vanilla bean ice cream.

6 Tbsp [85 g] cold unsalted butter, cut into ½-in [12-mm] cubes

1¾ cups [245 g] all-purpose flour

1 Tbsp baking powder

1 tsp kosher salt

½ cup plus 2 Tbsp [150 ml] cold whipping cream

3 Tbsp wildflower or orange blossom honey

2 tsp minced fresh or dried culinary lavender buds

1) In a large bowl, toss the butter cubes with 1 Tbsp of the flour until evenly coated. Transfer the coated butter to a small bowl and place in the freezer for about 10 minutes while you prepare the other ingredients.

2) In the same large bowl, whisk together the remaining flour, baking powder, and salt. In a small bowl, whisk together the cream, honey, and lavender until the honey is completely incorporated into the cream.

3) Remove the butter from the freezer, add to the flour mixture, and use a wooden spoon or rubber spatula to toss gently. Using a pastry cutter or two knives, cut the butter into the flour mixture until marble-size chunks of butter are visible. (Alternatively, in the bowl of a food processor fitted with the metal blade, cut the butter into the flour mixture with about three 1-second pulses.)

4) Add the buttermilk mixture to the flour mixture and toss gently with the wooden spoon or rubber spatula until the dough just starts to clump together. It will be shaggy and quite dry, and you should still see chunks of butter. Right about now you're likely to be thinking that there's a typo in the recipe or that I'm completely insane. Don't worry; it's going to work out, I promise! Cover the bowl with plastic wrap and place in the refrigerator for 30 minutes to allow the flour to hydrate.

5) Dust a large clean cutting board or counter with flour (a Silpat-style baking mat works well for this). Remove the bowl of dough from the refrigerator and scrape out the dough and any dry floury bits sticking

CONT'D

to the bowl onto the board. Coat your hands with flour and then pat the dough into a rectangle about ¾ in [2 cm] thick, with the long side approximately twice as long as the short side. Starting at one of the short ends, carefully fold the dough into thirds, like a business letter (a bench scraper is a handy tool for folding and for squaring off the sides and corners). It's fine if the dough isn't really holding together well and is breaking up; just pat it gently back into place and keep going. After turning the dough so that the short (open) end is facing you, use your hands to press the layers together gently and neaten the dough to restore its rectangular shape. Then use a rolling pin to roll the dough into a ½-in- [12-mm-] thick rectangle, and repeat the folding and gentle pressing. Repeat the turning, rolling, and folding one more time, for a total of 3 times, and then roll the dough into an approximately 4-by-8¾-in [10-by-22-cm] rectangle. Wrap the dough in plastic wrap and refrigerate for at least 30 minutes or up to 24 hours.

6) Preheat the oven to 400°F [200°C]. Line a baking sheet with parchment paper or coat with nonstick cooking spray.

7) Remove the dough from the refrigerator, trim about ½ in [12 mm] off the edges of the rectangle, and then, using a large sharp knife dipped in flour after each cut, cut the rectangle into 8 equal pieces. (I like to roll the trimmed bits into a tight spiral, pinch the ends together, and bake those as well.) Place the pieces on the prepared baking sheet, spacing them at least 1 in [2.5 cm] apart.

8) Bake for 5 minutes, then lower the oven temperature to 375°F [190°C] and rotate the pan. Bake until puffed and golden brown on top, 8 to 10 minutes more.

9) Transfer the biscuits to a wire rack to cool for 5 minutes. If you are not serving the biscuits right away, wrap them tightly in plastic or place them in a resealable bag and store in the freezer for up to 1 month. To serve, place the biscuits on a baking sheet and warm in a preheated 400°F [200°C] oven for 5 minutes.

HAM, THYME, AND ORANGE ZEST

BISCUITS

MAKES TEN 2-IN [5-CM] BISCUITS

This may sound like an unusual combination of flavors, but trust me, it's sophisticated and delicious. The sweet meaty ham chunks, herbal and heady thyme, and fruity zest play off each other to make a unique biscuit with a heavenly aroma. If you can get fresh lemon thyme, a unique varietal with unusual citrus notes, try this recipe with it.

2 cups [240 g] all-purpose flour

2 tsp sugar

2½ tsp baking powder

1½ tsp kosher salt

1½ cups [360 ml] heavy cream

1 Tbsp minced fresh thyme leaves (do not use dried thyme)

1 Tbsp grated orange zest (about 1 large orange)

6 oz [170 g] cured ham (the type you'd eat for breakfast), cut into ¼-in [6-mm] pieces

2 Tbsp salted butter, melted (optional)

1) Preheat the oven to 475°F [240°C]. Line a baking sheet with parchment paper or coat with nonstick cooking spray.

2) In a medium bowl, whisk together the flour, sugar, baking powder, and salt. In a small bowl, whisk together the cream, thyme, and orange zest. Add the cream mixture and the diced ham to the flour mixture and use a wooden spoon or rubber spatula to stir, scraping the sides of the bowl as you go, just until the dough forms a ball, about 30 seconds. Scrape the biscuit dough out onto a lightly floured board. Dust your hands with flour and knead the dough 8 times, folding it back onto itself and rotating the ball a quarter turn (90 degrees) each time. Working your way from the center out, use a rolling pin or pat the dough ball with your hands into a round about ¾ in [2 cm] thick, dusting with additional flour if the dough begins to stick to your hands or the board.

3) Using a biscuit cutter dipped in flour between each cut, cut as many biscuits as you can. Gather the scraps, if any, gently pat out again, and cut additional biscuits. Do not twist the biscuit cutter while cutting; this prevents maximum rise by sealing the edges together. (If you don't have a biscuit cutter, dip a sharp knife in flour and divide the dough into 10 equal chunks. Don't worry too much about the shape; they will expand in the oven.)

CONT'D

4) Place the biscuits on the prepared baking sheet, spacing them about 1 in [2.5 cm] apart. (At this point, you can store the unbaked biscuits, covered tightly with plastic wrap on the baking sheet, in the refrigerator for up to 24 hours.)

5) Bake until puffed and golden brown, rotating the baking sheet halfway through, about 12 minutes. If you like, brush the hot biscuits with the melted butter after removing them from the oven. This gives the biscuits a shiny top and a little extra richness.

6) Transfer the biscuits to a wire rack to cool for 5 minutes. If you are not serving the biscuits right away, wrap them tightly in plastic or place in a resealable bag and store in the freezer for up to 1 month. To serve, place the biscuits on a baking sheet and warm in a preheated 400°F [200°C] oven for 5 minutes.

DILL AND ONION WHOLE-WHEAT BISCUITS

MAKES TWELVE 2-IN [5-CM] BISCUITS

This recipe is similar in style to the Cathead Biscuits on page 101: it makes very soft and shaggy dough that's coated thickly in flour and butter before baking. The result is a soft, fluffy biscuit inside with a thick crunchy crust on top. These whole-wheat biscuits rise up nice and high and aren't weighed down by the whole wheat. The dill and onion add texture and flavor that complements the nuttiness of the whole wheat.

4 Tbsp [55 g] cold unsalted butter, plus 3 Tbsp [40 g], melted and cooled

2 tsp vegetable oil

1 small yellow onion, quartered and very thinly sliced

1⅔ cups [230 g] all-purpose flour

¾ cup [105 g] whole-wheat flour

1 Tbsp sugar

1 Tbsp baking powder

½ tsp baking soda

2 tsp kosher salt

2 Tbsp chopped fresh dill or 1 Tbsp dried dill

1½ cups [360 ml] cold buttermilk

1) Preheat the oven to 475°F [240°C]. Butter or coat with nonstick cooking spray a 9-in [23-cm] round cake pan or an 8-by-8-in [20-by-20-cm] square baking dish.

2) Cut 4 Tbsp [55 g] of the butter into ½-in [12-mm] cubes. Place them in a small bowl and put them in the freezer for at least 10 minutes while you prepare the other ingredients.

3) In a large nonstick skillet over medium-low heat, warm the oil and swirl to coat the pan. Add the onion and cook, stirring frequently with a rubber spatula or wooden spoon, until all the onion slices are lightly browned and cooked through, about 8 minutes. Remove from the heat and set aside to cool.

4) Place ⅓ cup [45 g] of the flour in a wide, shallow bowl (another cake pan or baking dish works well) and shake gently to distribute evenly. Set aside.

5) In a medium bowl, whisk together the remaining 1⅓ cups [180 g] all-purpose flour, whole-wheat flour, sugar, baking powder, baking soda, and salt. In a small bowl, stir the dill and cooked onion into the buttermilk. Cover the buttermilk mixture with plastic wrap and refrigerate until ready to use.

6) Using a pastry cutter or two knives, cut the frozen butter into the flour mixture until no pieces larger than a pea remain. (Alternatively, in the bowl of a food processor fitted with the metal blade, cut the frozen butter into the flour mixture with five 1-second pulses.) Return the mixture to the medium bowl.

7) Add the buttermilk mixture, and use a wooden spoon or rubber spatula to stir just until no streaks of flour are visible, about 20 strokes. The dough will be wet, lumpy, and shaggy.

8) Using a large serving spoon, drop two or three large scoops of dough into the reserved ⅓ cup [45 g] flour. Dust your hands with flour and very gently roll each scoop in the flour until fully coated. Place the floured scoops closely together in the prepared pan. Repeat until all the dough is used. You should have about 12 dough balls. Sprinkle any remaining flour over the dough balls in the pan and gently brush them with the 3 Tbsp melted butter.

9) Bake until puffed and golden brown, rotating the pan halfway through, about 15 minutes.

10) Transfer the pan to a wire rack to cool for 5 minutes before turning out onto a plate. (Here's a trick for this: Place a dinner plate upside down over the pan, then use two kitchen towels or hot pads to grip the sides of the pan and plate together; quickly flip over, set the plate on a countertop, and remove the pan. Then place another dinner plate on top of what it now the bottom of the biscuits and repeat the flip so your biscuits are right-side-up.) If you are not serving the biscuits right away, wrap them tightly in plastic or place in a resealable bag and store in the freezer for up to 1 month. To serve, place the biscuits on a baking sheet and warm in a preheated 400°F [200°C] oven for 5 minutes.

BUCKWHEAT GRUYÈRE
BISCUITS

MAKES TEN 2½-IN [6-CM] BISCUITS

The slightly sweet, nutty flavor of buckwheat is perfectly offset by rich Gruyère cheese in these light, fluffy, buttermilk biscuits. Buckwheat has no gluten, which is the stuff that makes bread chewy when you use wheat flour, so the buckwheat flour contributes to the tenderness of the biscuit. Tarragon is a lovely herb that tastes of anise and adds an interesting bit of complexity to the flavor profile of these biscuits.

¾ cup [165 g] cold unsalted butter, cut into ½-in [12-mm] cubes, plus 1 Tbsp, melted and cooled

1½ cups [140 g] shredded Gruyère cheese

1 cup [140 g] buckwheat flour

2 cups [280 g] all-purpose flour

1 Tbsp baking powder

1 tsp baking soda

2 tsp kosher salt

1¼ cups [300 ml] buttermilk

2 Tbsp firmly packed brown sugar

1½ cups [140 g] shredded Gruyère cheese

2 Tbsp (4 or 5 sprigs) chopped fresh tarragon or 2 tsp dried tarragon (optional)

Freshly ground black pepper

1) Place the ¾ cup [165 g] butter in a small bowl and place in the freezer for about 10 minutes while you prepare the other ingredients. Set aside 1 Tbsp of the Gruyère in a small bowl for the biscuit topping.

2) In the bowl of a food processer fitted with the metal blade, place the buckwheat flour, all-purpose flour, baking powder, baking soda, and salt. Pulse briefly to mix. If you do not have a food processor, whisk together in a large bowl. In a small bowl, whisk together the buttermilk and brown sugar until well combined.

3) Scatter the frozen butter pieces on top of the flour mixture in the food processor and pulse for five 1-second increments, or until the butter is just cut in and some butter pieces are still visible. (Alternatively, cut the butter into the flour mixture with a pastry cutter or two knives.)

4) Place the flour mixture into a large bowl and add the buttermilk mixture, the remaining shredded cheese, and the tarragon (if using). Stir with a wooden spoon or rubber spatula just until the dough comes together, about 20 seconds. The dough will be quite stiff. Scrape the biscuit dough out onto a lightly floured board. Dust your hands with flour and gather the dough into a ball. Knead the dough 8 times, folding it back onto itself and rotating the ball a quarter

CONT'D

turn each time, dusting with additional flour if the dough sticks to your hands or the board. Place the dough back into the bowl, cover tightly with plastic wrap, and refrigerate for 30 minutes.

5) While the dough is resting in the refrigerator, preheat the oven to 475°F [240°C]. Line a baking sheet with parchment paper or coat with nonstick cooking spray.

6) Remove the dough from the refrigerator and turn it out onto a lightly floured board. Working your way from the center out, gently pat with your hands or use a rolling pin to roll the dough ball into a round disk about ¾ in [2 cm] thick, dusting with additional flour if the dough begins to stick to your hands or the board. Using a biscuit cutter dipped in flour between each cut, cut as many biscuits out of the disk as possible. Gather the dough scraps, if any, and pat or roll out for more biscuits if necessary. Do not twist the biscuit cutter while cutting; this prevents maximum rise by sealing the edges together. (If you don't have a biscuit cutter, dip a sharp knife in flour and divide the dough into 10 equal chunks. Don't worry too much about the shape: they will expand in the oven.)

7) Place the biscuits on the prepared baking sheet, spacing them about 1 in [2.5 cm] apart, and brush the tops with the 1 Tbsp melted butter. Sprinkle the reserved shredded cheese evenly over the biscuits and then lightly dust them with freshly ground black pepper.

8) Bake for 5 minutes, then lower the heat to 400°F [200°C] and continue baking until puffed and golden brown, rotating the baking sheet halfway through, about 10 minutes more.

9) Transfer the biscuits to a wire rack to cool for 5 minutes. If you are not serving the biscuits right away, wrap them tightly in plastic or place in a resealable bag and store in the freezer for up to 1 month. To serve, place the biscuits on a baking sheet and warm in a preheated 400°F [200°C] oven for 5 minutes.

ROSEMARY-PARMESAN PINWHEEL
BISCUITS

MAKES SIXTEEN 2-IN [5-CM] BISCUITS

The first time I brought a batch of these crunchy, flaky biscuit spirals to a dinner party, they disappeared before the welcoming cocktails had even been poured. These tasty and pretty biscuits contain a swirl of earthy Parmesan and fragrant rosemary, but you can use almost any combination of hard cheese and herb you wish. Because the recipe calls for making two separate rolls, you can also mix-'n'-match and make two different flavors at the same time, so that there's something for everyone.

1 recipe Ultra-Flaky Biscuit dough (page 107)

3 cups [90 g] grated Parmesan cheese

2 Tbsp minced fresh rosemary or 1 Tbsp dried rosemary

1) Preheat the oven to 400°F [200°C]. Line two baking sheets with parchment paper or coat with nonstick cooking spray.

2) Dust a clean countertop or large cutting board with flour. Cut the rectangle of biscuit dough in half and return one half to the refrigerator while you work with the other. Using a rolling pin, roll the dough out to an 8-by-16-in [20-by-40-cm] rectangle, dusting with additional flour as necessary to keep the dough from sticking.

3) Sprinkle half the cheese evenly across the surface of the dough, leaving a ½-in [12-mm] clear strip along one long edge. Sprinkle half the rosemary evenly over the cheese. Starting at the edge opposite the clear strip, tightly roll the dough, tucking in any cheese that falls out and pressing the log into an even shape as you roll. When you get to the far edge, moisten the clear strip with water by dipping your finger in cold water and then run your wet finger along the strip. Finish rolling up the dough, smoothing the moistened strip against the dough to help it stick and gently squeezing the roll from end to end to get it into an even, firmly rolled shape.

4) With a sharp knife dipped in flour, cut the roll crosswise in half. Cut one half crosswise into 4 pieces. Cut each of those pieces in half to make 8 pieces. Be sure to dip the knife in flour after each cut. Place the biscuits on the prepared baking sheet cut-side-up, spacing them at least 1 in [2.5 cm] apart. Repeat with the second half of biscuit dough and place the second set of biscuits on the second prepared baking sheet.

CONT'D

5) Bake until puffed and golden brown, rotating the baking sheets halfway through, 18 to 20 minutes. Don't worry if some of the spirals loosen a bit in the oven; these little spiral biscuit arms will be extra crunchy and delicious.

6) Transfer the biscuits to a wire rack to cool for 5 minutes. If you are not serving the biscuits right away, wrap them tightly in plastic or place in a resealable bag and store in the freezer for up to 1 month. To serve, place the biscuits on a baking sheet and warm in a preheated 400°F [200°C] oven for 5 minutes.

 *Variations*

Chile-Cheddar: Substitute 2 cups [160 g] shredded medium or sharp Cheddar for the Parmesan and 2 tsp chile powder for the rosemary.

Sage-Gruyère: Substitute 2 cups [160 g] shredded Gruyère for the Parmesan and 2 Tbsp minced fresh sage (or 1 Tbsp dried rubbed sage) for the rosemary.

CHEDDAR-BACON
BISCUITS

MAKES EIGHT 2½-IN [6-CM] BISCUITS

These biscuits use the same technique as that for Cathead Biscuits (page 101), but they are enriched with egg, sharp Cheddar cheese, and crispy bacon. With a nice crisp top crust and a soft interior, they're hearty enough to serve as breakfast on their own, or you can make them the centerpiece of a farmhouse-style brunch spread.

¾ cup [105 g] all-purpose flour, plus 2 Tbsp

¾ cup [90 g] cake flour

1½ tsp baking powder

¼ tsp baking soda

1 tsp kosher salt

½ tsp freshly ground black pepper

6 Tbsp [85 g] cold unsalted butter, cut into ¼-in [6-mm] cubes, plus 2 Tbsp, melted and cooled

1½ cups [115 g] shredded Cheddar cheese

8 slices thick-cut bacon, cooked until crisp, drained, and cut into ½-in [12-mm] pieces

1 egg

½ cup [120 ml] cold buttermilk

1) Preheat the oven to 400°F [200°C]. Coat a 9-by-5-in [23-by-12-cm] loaf pan with nonstick cooking spray.

2) In a large bowl, whisk together the ¾ cup [105 g] all-purpose flour, cake flour, baking powder, baking soda, salt, and pepper. Scatter the butter cubes over the flour mixture and use a wooden spoon or rubber spatula to toss gently. Using a pastry cutter or two knives, cut the butter into the flour until the mixture resembles coarse meal but pea-size chunks of butter are still visible. (Alternatively, in the bowl of a food processor fitted with a metal blade, cut the butter into the flour mixture with about three 1-second pulses, and then return the mixture to the mixing bowl.) Reserve 2 Tbsp shredded Cheddar for the topping and set aside. Using a wooden spoon or rubber spatula, stir the remaining Cheddar and the chopped bacon into the flour mixture.

3) In a small bowl, whisk the egg and buttermilk together until blended. Add the buttermilk mixture to the flour mixture and, using a wooden spoon or rubber spatula, stir until the dough just comes together, scraping down the sides of the bowl as needed. The dough should be shaggy and a little sticky.

CONT'D

4) Spoon the remaining 2 Tbsp all-purpose flour into a shallow bowl. Coat your hands well with flour and pull off egg-size chunks of dough (you want 8 biscuits, so aim for dough balls that are one-eighth of the total). Dredge each chunk in the flour until thoroughly coated and place them in the prepared pan so that they are barely touching (2 biscuits across the shorter width of the bread pan and 4 biscuits along the longer side, for a 2-by-4 grid of 8 biscuits). Resist the urge to smooth and shape the dough; leave it rough and shaggy. Dust any remaining flour over the biscuits in the pan.

5) Brush the tops of the biscuits with the melted butter, pouring any remaining butter over them. Sprinkle the reserved Cheddar evenly over the biscuits.

6) Bake until puffed and golden brown, rotating the loaf pan halfway through, about 20 minutes.

7) Transfer the biscuits to a wire rack to cool for 5 minutes and serve warm. If you are not serving the biscuits right away, wrap them tightly in plastic or place in a resealable bag and store in the freezer for up to 1 month. To serve, place the biscuits on a baking sheet and warm in a preheated 400°F [200°C] oven for 5 minutes.

GREEN CHILE-CORNMEAL
BISCUITS

MAKES TWELVE 2½-IN [6-CM] BISCUITS

These golden gems, flecked with red bell pepper and green chiles, couldn't look more festive or appetizing. A delicious alternative to plain corn bread, which is often overly sweet as well as dry, these tender spicy biscuits are perfect for a summer barbecue. Soaking the cornmeal in buttermilk softens it and makes the biscuit less gritty. Egg yolk gives them their unusually bright yellow color and also increases their moisture, so they will be crunchy on the edges but soft and fluffy in the middle. Serve them hot and fresh out of the oven; as the biscuits cool, the chiles release moisture, and the biscuits lose their crunch. Look for yellow whole-kernel and finely ground cornmeal or corn flour; the more widely available cornmeal, from which the germ has been removed, will not yield the best flavor.

¾ cup [105 g] finely ground stone-ground cornmeal or corn flour

¾ cup [180 ml] buttermilk, plus up to 2 Tbsp (if needed)

1 Tbsp wildflower or orange blossom honey

1 egg yolk

1¾ cups [245 g] all-purpose flour

2¼ tsp baking powder

¾ tsp baking soda

2 tsp kosher salt

9 Tbsp [130 g] cold unsalted butter, cut into ½-in [12-mm] cubes

1 small red bell pepper, stem, ribs, and seeds removed, cut into ¼-in [6-mm] pieces

1 green jalapeño chile, stem and seeds removed, cut into ¼-in [6-mm] pieces

1) Preheat the oven to 425°F [220°C]. Line a baking sheet with parchment or coat with nonstick cooking spray.

2) In a large bowl, whisk together the cornmeal, buttermilk, honey, and egg yolk. Set aside for 10 minutes while you prepare the other ingredients.

3) In a medium bowl, whisk together the flour, baking powder, baking soda, and salt. Using a pastry cutter or two knives, cut in the butter until the mixture resembles coarse sand and no pieces of butter larger than small peas remain. (Alternatively, in the bowl of a food processor fitted with the metal blade, cut the butter into the flour mixture with about five 1-second pulses.)

CONT'D

4) Stir the bell pepper and jalapeño into the cornmeal mixture, then add the flour mixture and use a wooden spoon or rubber spatula to stir until just combined. The dough will be stiff. If it won't clump together, stir in more buttermilk, 1 Tbsp at a time, and then squeeze the dough with your hands to form it into a ball.

5) Turn the dough out onto a floured cutting board or countertop and knead with floured hands, adding flour as necessary to prevent sticking, about 10 times, or just until a smooth dough forms. Working your way from the center out, gently pat with your hands or use a rolling pin to roll the dough ball into a round disk about ¾ in [2 cm] thick, dusting with additional flour if the dough begins to stick to your hands or the board.

6) Using a biscuit cutter dipped in flour between each cut, cut as many biscuits out of the disk as possible. Gather the dough scraps and pat or roll out to cut more biscuits. Do not twist the biscuit cutter while cutting; this prevents maximum rise by sealing the edges together. (If you don't have a biscuit cutter, dip a sharp knife in flour and divide the dough into 12 equal chunks.) Place the biscuits on the prepared baking sheet, spacing them at least 1 in [2.5 cm] apart.

7) Bake until the biscuits are puffed and the tops are an even golden brown, rotating the pan halfway through, 10 to 12 minutes.

8) Transfer the biscuits to a wire rack to cool for 5 minutes. If you are not serving the biscuits right away, wrap them tightly in plastic or place in a resealable bag and store in the freezer for up to 1 month. To serve, place the biscuits on a baking sheet and warm in a preheated 400°F [200°C] oven for 5 minutes.

BISCUIT 'N' EGGS

SERVES 1

This is a very flexible recipe for a quintessential breakfast classic. For our version, we start with a perfect, fluffy grilled biscuit, and then we pile on some cheese, bacon, and egg. This is a basic open-faced biscuit sandwich, but we offer a host of delicious dough variations. You can also experiment with different cheeses and layer on complementary ingredients like tomatoes, sautéed vegetables, and thinly sliced cooked meats. Finally, I like my eggs over easy, but you can substitute almost any egg preparation you prefer; scrambled, over hard, and poached eggs all work great. The cream biscuits are also delicious for dinner. If you manage to have any left over, you'll have the beginnings of a glorious breakfast the next day.

1 tsp vegetable oil

2 eggs

Kosher salt and freshly ground black pepper

1 Perfectly Easy Cream Biscuit (page 99), split in half horizontally

2 slices mild, medium, or sharp Cheddar cheese

2 strips bacon, cut in half, cooked until crisp, and drained, or 2 slices cooked Canadian bacon

1) In a medium nonstick skillet over medium-low heat, warm the vegetable oil and swirl the pan to coat. Carefully crack both eggs into the pan and sprinkle with salt and pepper.

2) Place the biscuit halves cut-side-down in the skillet next to the eggs. After about 1 minute, or when the egg whites are mostly cooked through, carefully flip the eggs with a silicone spatula. (Don't worry if you break a yolk; it will still taste good.) Cook the eggs until the egg whites are fully cooked but the yolks are still soft, about 30 seconds longer. Remove the pan from the heat.

3) Transfer the biscuit halves cut-side-up to a plate. Place a slice of cheese on top of each biscuit half while they are still warm. Top the cheese on both biscuit halves with 2 half-strips of bacon each and then slide a fried egg on top of each biscuit stack. Serve immediately.

BISCUIT BREAKFAST SANDWICH

SERVES 1

Leftover biscuits make a fantastic and quick breakfast sandwich the next morning. This version, made with fresh spicy Spanish chorizo, a slice of ripe tomato, and an over-easy egg, is my personal favorite, but any kind of sausage patty will work well. You can add fresh spinach or baby arugula, grilled onions, or a smear of stone-ground mustard if you wish, and any good melting cheese, such as Cheddar, fontina, or Swiss will be divine.

1 tsp vegetable oil

2 oz [55 g] loose raw fresh chorizo sausage, formed into a patty about the same diameter as the biscuit and about ¼ in [6 mm] thick

1 egg

Kosher salt and freshly ground black pepper

2 slices Cheddar or pepper Jack cheese

1 Perfectly Easy Cream Biscuit (page 99) or Angel Biscuit (page 105), split in half horizontally

One ¼-in- [6-mm-] thick slice ripe tomato

1) In a medium nonstick skillet over medium-low heat, warm the oil and swirl the pan to coat. Add the sausage patty to the pan and cook until lightly browned on the bottom, about 2 minutes. Flip the patty over and carefully crack the egg into the pan next to the patty. Sprinkle the egg with salt and pepper. Place a slice of cheese on top of the chorizo patty so that it melts while the chorizo and egg finish cooking.

2) Place the biscuit halves cut-side-down in the skillet next to the egg and sausage (if you don't have room, you can warm the biscuit halves in the skillet after the egg and sausage are done). After about 1 minute, or when the egg white is mostly cooked through, carefully flip the egg with a silicone spatula. (Don't worry if you break the yolk, it will still taste good.) Cook the egg until the white is fully cooked but the yolk is still soft, about another 30 seconds. Remove the pan from the heat. Transfer the bottom biscuit half, cut-side-up, to a plate.

3) Place the second slice of cheese on top of the biscuit bottom while it is still warm. Place the chorizo patty on top of the cheese, and then top the patty with the tomato slice. Using a silicone spatula, carefully slide the fried egg on top of the tomato. Finally, top the stack with the remaining biscuit half, cut-side-down. Serve immediately.

BAKLAVA CINNAMON ROLLS

MAKES TWELVE 2½-IN [6-CM] ROLLS

I remember the first time I had baklava, a sweet, crunchy Middle Eastern pastry with layers of nuts between flaky, buttery sheets of phyllo drenched in honey syrup. I think baklava may have actually been my first true love, and I've been obsessed with it ever since. These biscuits have the familiar format of cinnamon rolls but with the exotic flavors of baklava.

SYRUP

¼ cup [60 ml] floral honey, such as wildflower or orange blossom honey

½ cup [100 g] sugar

½ cup [120 ml] water

4 whole cloves

1 cinnamon stick

Rind of 1 lemon, cut into 1-in [2.5-cm] strips (a vegetable peeler is handy for removing the rind, but make sure there is no bitter white pith attached)

1 Tbsp orange blossom water

FILLING

8 oz [230 g] raw pistachio nuts, finely chopped

8 oz [230 g] walnut pieces, finely chopped

1 cup [200 g] sugar

1 Tbsp ground cinnamon

¼ tsp ground cloves

4 Tbsp [55 g] salted butter, melted and cooled

1 recipe Angel Biscuit dough (page 105)

1) To make the syrup: In a small saucepan, whisk together the honey, sugar, water, whole cloves, cinnamon stick, and lemon rind and bring to a simmer over medium heat. Lower the heat slightly and let simmer gently for 15 minutes. Remove from the heat and stir in the orange blossom water. Set aside to allow the spices to steep.

2) To make the filling: In a medium mixing bowl, stir together the pistachios, walnuts, sugar, ground cinnamon, ground cloves, and melted butter.

3) Preheat the oven to 375°F [190°C]. Coat each well of a 12-well muffin pan with butter or nonstick cooking spray. Do not use muffin liners.

4) On a large clean cutting board or countertop dusted with flour, roll out the biscuit dough with a rolling pin into an 8-by-16-in [20-by-40-cm] rectangle, dusting with additional flour as needed to keep the dough from sticking. Sprinkle the filling evenly over the dough, leaving a ½-in [12-mm] clean strip along one of the long edges. Starting at the side opposite the clean strip, roll the dough tightly, just up to the clean strip. Dip your finger in cold water and moisten the clean strip, then smooth the edges together to seal. Gently squeeze the roll into an even shape.

5) With a sharp knife dipped in flour, cut the roll crosswise in half. Cut the halves crosswise into quarters and then each quarter into 3 equal pieces, wiping and dipping the knife in flour after each cut, so that you have 12 evenly sized biscuits. Place each piece in a muffin well, using your hands to gently reshape the pieces if they get squished a bit while cutting.

6) Bake until the tops are evenly browned and the rolls are firm to the touch, 18 to 20 minutes.

7) Spoon about 2 Tbsp syrup over each roll (while still in the muffin wells) and let sit for 2 to 3 minutes. Remove the rolls from the pan, using a butter knife to help lift the rolls from the pan if needed and spooning any syrup that collects in the wells back over the rolls after removing, and serve immediately. Pass any extra syrup on the side.

FIG-CHUTNEY BREAKFAST ROLLS

MAKES TWELVE 2-IN [5-CM] BISCUITS

This is a sophisticated breakfast roll, sweet but tart and intensely flavorful. It is made with buttery, crunchy biscuit dough that provides the gingery fig chutney with a perfect foil. Because this recipe calls for splitting a batch of Ultra-Flaky Biscuit dough in half to make 2 rolls, I like to make one half into savory Pinwheel Biscuits (page 123) for dinner and the other half into Fig-Chutney Breakfast Rolls for breakfast the next morning.

½ recipe Ultra-Flaky Biscuit dough (page 107)

1¼ cups [300 ml] Fig and Orange Chutney (page 157)

1) Preheat the oven to 375°F [190°C]. Coat each well of a 12-well muffin pan with nonstick cooking spray. I do not recommend using paper liners; the biscuits will not form a crunchy crust.

2) On a large clean cutting board or countertop dusted with flour, roll out the dough with a rolling pin into an 8-by-16-in [20-by-40-cm] rectangle, dusting with additional flour as needed to keep the dough from sticking. Spread half of the chutney evenly over the dough, leaving a clean ½-in [12-mm] strip along one of the long edges. Starting at the side opposite the clean strip, roll the dough tightly only as far as the edge of the clean strip. Dip your finger in cold water and moisten the clean strip, then smooth the edges together to seal. Gently squeeze the roll into an even shape.

3) With a sharp knife dipped in flour, cut the roll crosswise in half. Cut the halves crosswise in half again, for 4 equal pieces, and then each quarter into 3 equal pieces, wiping and dipping the knife in flour after each cut, so that you have 12 evenly sized biscuits. Place each piece in a muffin well, using your hands to gently reshape the pieces if they get squished a bit while cutting.

4) Bake until the tops are evenly browned and the biscuits are firm to the touch, 18 to 20 minutes.

5) Transfer to a wire rack and let the biscuits cool in the pan for about 5 minutes. Then remove from the muffin wells, using a butter knife if needed to help lift the biscuits out of the pan, and cool for another 5 minutes before serving.

INDIVIDUAL
MONKEY BREAD
with PECANS and BOURBON SAUCE

MAKES TWELVE 2½-IN [6-CM] MONKEY BREADS

Quick show of hands: who here knows what monkey bread is? Truth is, I didn't need to see your hands; if you've had this fun treat, then you're already grinning at the memory of it and I can tell by the look on your face. Monkey breads are pull-apart cinnamon rolls: gooey, sweet, and decadent. You can serve them as a dessert or as part of an indulgent brunch. Children go especially bananas for monkey bread not only because it's a delicious treat but also because you get to eat it with your hands. If you want to make this recipe kid-friendly, just leave out the bourbon in the sauce and enlist their help: they'll have fun shaping the dough, dunking the balls in the butter, and rolling them in the cinnamon-sugar.

¾ cup [80 g] coarsely chopped pecans (optional)

1 cup [200 g] sugar

1 Tbsp ground cinnamon

1 recipe Angel Biscuit dough (page 105)

5 Tbsp [60 g] unsalted butter, melted and cooled slightly

1 recipe Brown Sugar–Bourbon Sauce (page 160)

1) Preheat the oven to 350°F [180°C]. Butter or coat each well of a 12-well muffin pan with nonstick cooking spray and spoon 1 Tbsp pecans into the bottom of each well, if desired. Do not use muffin liners.

2) In a medium bowl, stir together the sugar and cinnamon until well mixed. Set aside.

3) Pinch off 5 small chunks of biscuit dough and roll each quickly and gently between your hands to form balls about ¾ in [2 cm] in diameter. Dunk the dough balls in the melted butter and then roll them in the cinnamon-sugar until thoroughly coated (I like to use both hands and do two balls at a time). Place all 5 balls in a prepared muffin well, on top of the pecans, if using. Don't worry about fitting them evenly into the cup; they'll expand and even out as they bake. Repeat with the remaining dough to fill the remaining muffin wells. If you end up with any extra dough, use it to make additional balls and add them to any wells that look a little low. Drizzle ½ cup [120 ml] of the bourbon sauce evenly over all the muffin wells, about 2 tsp per well.

CONT'D

4) Bake until the tops are evenly browned and the breads are firm to the touch, 18 to 22 minutes, or poke a small sharp knife into the center of one bread to see if it comes out clean.

5) Transfer to a wire rack and place a clean, dry cutting board that is at least as large as the muffin pan facedown on the muffin pan. Using pot holders or two towels, grip the edges of the pan and the cutting board together and carefully flip both of them over so that the muffin pan is facedown on top of the cutting board. Let cool in the pan for 5 minutes and then carefully lift the muffin pan off the cutting board. (If a few pecans stick in the muffin wells, just scoop them out with a spoon and tuck them back into place on the monkey breads.)

6) Drizzle each monkey bread with about 2 tsp of the remaining Brown Sugar–Bourbon Sauce and serve warm.

Variation

Bundt-Pan Monkey Bread: To make a traditional monkey bread baked in a large Bundt pan, coat the pan with nonstick cooking spray and then sprinkle half of the pecans in the bottom of the pan. Place half the coated dough balls on top of the pecans, then top with the remaining pecans and then the remaining dough balls. Drizzle half of the Brown Sugar–Bourbon Sauce over the Bundt pan and increase the baking time to about 40 minutes. Check with a cake tester or sharp knife to make sure the monkey bread is cooked all the way through. Let cool in the pan for 5 minutes, then unmold onto a serving plate and drizzle with the remaining Brown Sugar–Bourbon Sauce.

PISTACHIO-STRAWBERRY SHORTCAKES

WITH WHITE CHOCOLATE CREAM

SERVES 6

These aren't your mother's strawberry shortcakes. Well, not unless your mother is a pastry chef. You can start this scene-stealing dessert two days before serving and bake and assemble it at the last minute: the white chocolate cream (before you beat in the whipped cream) can be made two days in advance, and the shortcake dough and sliced berries can sit in the refrigerator overnight. You can use fresh raspberries, blackberries, or a combination of berries in place of the strawberries. The pistachio shortcakes are delicious on their own, or you can serve them with Meyer Lemon Curd (page 155) or Strawberry Butter (page 151) for a sophisticated addition to a weekend brunch.

WHITE CHOCOLATE CREAM

1 Tbsp sugar

1 egg yolk

⅓ cup [60 g] white chocolate chips

1 cup [240 ml] cold heavy whipping cream

¼ tsp vanilla extract

¼ cup [80 ml] sour cream or crème fraîche

STRAWBERRIES

1½ lb [680 g] fresh ripe strawberries

½ cup [120 ml] Fresh Strawberry Preserves (page 165)

3 Tbsp white chocolate chips

½ tsp canola oil

1 Tbsp finely chopped pistachios

PISTACHIO SHORTCAKES

½ cup [110 g] cold unsalted butter, plus 1 Tbsp, melted and slightly cooled

2 cups [280 g] all-purpose flour

½ cup [60 g] plus 2 tsp finely chopped pistachios

¼ cup [50 g] plus 1 Tbsp sugar

1 Tbsp baking powder

1 tsp kosher salt

1 egg

½ cup plus 1 Tbsp [135 ml] cold heavy cream

1) To make the cream: In a small bowl, whisk together the sugar and egg yolk until well combined. Place the white chocolate chips in a medium

CONT'D

heat-resistant bowl. In a small nonreactive saucepan over medium heat, bring ½ cup [120 ml] of the cream to a boil, then immediately turn off the heat.

2) Whisk one-third of the hot cream into the egg yolk mixture, then scrape all of the egg yolk mixture back into the hot cream in the saucepan and whisk vigorously until blended. Turn the heat to medium-low and continue to cook, stirring constantly with a heat-resistant rubber spatula, until the mixture thickens or reaches 180°F [82°C] on a candy thermometer, about another 2 minutes.

3) Immediately remove the pan from the heat and pour through a fine-mesh strainer over the white chocolate chips. Discard any solids in the strainer. Let the mixture sit until the chocolate softens, about 2 minutes. Add the vanilla and stir with the rubber spatula until the chocolate is fully melted and fully incorporated into the cream. The mixture should be smooth and shiny. Cover tightly with plastic wrap and refrigerate until completely chilled, at least 1 hour or up to 2 days.

4) To prepare the strawberries: Select 6 of the prettiest berries and reserve them for garnish. Remove the stems from the remaining strawberries and cut them into ¼-in [6-mm] slices. Place the sliced strawberries in a medium bowl, add the preserves, and stir gently until the berries are evenly coated. Cover and let sit at room temperature for 2 hours, or up to 24 hours (refrigerate if sitting for more than 4 hours).

5) Place an 8-by-8-in [20-by-20-cm] square of parchment or foil on a plate and set aside. In a small microwave-safe bowl, microwave the white chocolate chips and canola oil at full power until the chips

begin to soften, 30 seconds. (They will continue to melt as you stir them, so watch carefully while they are in the microwave and remove the chips before they are melted, or they may burn.) Remove from the microwave and stir the mixture with a small metal spoon until smooth. If the chocolate is not completely melted after 30 seconds of stirring, microwave in 10-second increments, stirring between each increment, until melted.

6) Dip each of the reserved whole berries in the melted white chocolate, coating them nearly up to the stem, and immediately sprinkle with a pinch of the finely chopped pistachios. Place the coated berries on the parchment-covered plate and refrigerate while you prepare the other ingredients.

7) To make the shortcakes: Cut the ½ cup [110 g] butter into ½-in [12-mm] pieces and freeze for at least 10 minutes, or until ready to use. In a large bowl, whisk together the flour, ½ cup [60 g] of the pistachios, ¼ cup [50 g] of the sugar, baking powder, and salt. In a small bowl, whisk together the egg and cream.

8) Add the frozen butter to the flour mixture. Using a pastry cutter or two knives, cut in the butter until the mixture resembles coarse sand and a few visible chunks of butter remain. (Alternatively, in the bowl of a food processor fitted with the metal blade, cut the butter into the flour mixture with five 1-second pulses.)

9) Return the flour mixture to the large bowl, add the cream mixture, and use a wooden spoon or rubber spatula to stir until the dough just comes together. Dust a cutting board or clean countertop with flour, turn out the dough, and knead about

8 times, or just until a smooth ball forms. Return the dough ball to the bowl, cover tightly with plastic wrap, and refrigerate for 30 minutes.

10) While the dough is resting in the refrigerator, preheat the oven to 425°F [220°C]. Line a baking sheet with parchment paper or coat with nonstick cooking spray.

11) In a small bowl, stir the remaining 1 Tbsp sugar and 2 tsp chopped pistachios together.

12) Remove the dough from the refrigerator and turn it out onto a clean countertop or cutting board dusted with flour. Working your way from the center out, gently pat with your hands or use a rolling pin to roll the dough ball into a round disk about 1 in [2.5 cm] thick, adding flour as necessary to prevent sticking. Use a 3-in [7.5-cm] biscuit cutter to cut out as many shortcakes as possible, then gently gather the dough scraps and cut out as many additional shortcakes as possible. You should have 6. Place them on the prepared baking sheet, spacing them at least 1 in [2.5 cm] apart. Brush the shortcakes with the melted butter and sprinkle evenly with the sugar-pistachio mixture.

13) Bake until puffed and the tops are lightly browned, about 12 minutes.

14) Transfer to a wire rack and let cool in the pan for 10 minutes.

15) While the shortcakes are cooling, in a medium bowl with a handheld electric mixer or in a stand mixer with the whisk attachment, beat the chilled white chocolate cream, remaining ½ cup [120 ml] heavy whipping cream, and sour cream on high speed until stiff peaks form, about 2 minutes. For the fluffiest whipped cream, make sure that everything is very cold before starting. If your kitchen is hot, put the bowl and beaters in the freezer for 10 minutes before starting.

16) Carefully split the shortcakes horizontally in half with a sharp knife. Place the bottom half of one shortcake, split-side-up, on a small dessert plate. Mound one-sixth of the macerated strawberries on top (let a few berry slices fall decoratively onto the plate), then spoon one-sixth of the white chocolate cream on top of the berries (it's fine if the cream spills out onto the plate). Place the top half of the short-cake, split-side-down, on top of the stack. Garnish with a white chocolate–covered strawberry. Repeat with the remaining shortcakes. Serve immediately.

Variations

Pistachio-Strawberry Shortcakes with Dark Chocolate Cream: Substitute semisweet or bittersweet chocolate for the white chocolate. Increase the sugar in Step 1 by 1 Tbsp. The cream base will be quite stiff once it is chilled but will whip up fine with the heavy whipping cream and sour cream.

Pistachio-Strawberry Shortcakes with Lemon Cream: Skip Steps 1–3 (do not make the white chocolate cream base, so you can omit the White Chocolate Cream ingredients). In Step 15, combine ½ cup [120 ml] whipping cream, 6 Tbsp Meyer Lemon Curd (page 155, or use store-bought lemon curd), and ¼ cup [80 ml] sour cream in a medium bowl and whip as directed.

BISCUIT STRATA

SERVES 6

Strata is just a fancy word for a savory layered dish of bread, meats, cheeses, and egg custard that is baked until set. I believe that it may be the best brunch dish ever devised. Think of it as some crazy cross between a grilled cheese and a quiche. That sounds weird, but trust me, it is really delicious. Nate and I encountered our first breakfast strata many years back while we were on a houseboat trip in northern California with a bunch of old friends. One of the guests made a ham-and-cheese strata in advance of the trip and baked it right before brunch. Soft, warm, savory, and delicious—it was a revelation, and we resolved to make it our own.

For my version, I like to use day-old biscuits (on the rare day there are any left!), but any bread will work. You can use almost any cheese you have on hand, but the combination of Cheddar, fontina, and Gruyère is particularly delicious for this construction. Assemble the dish the night before, refrigerate it, and bake it the next morning for a stress-free and crowd-pleasing breakfast.

BISCUIT STRATA

3 day-old Perfectly Easy Cream Biscuits (page 99), Cathead Biscuits (page 101), Angel Biscuits (page 105), or Ultra-Flaky Biscuits (page 107), cut or torn into roughly 1-in [2.5-cm] cubes (see Note)

4 oz [115 g] loosely packed shredded cheese (mixed Cheddar, fontina, and Gruyère)

3 eggs, plus 4 egg yolks

½ tsp kosher salt

½ tsp freshly ground black pepper

¼ tsp garlic powder

1 tsp minced fresh thyme

Pinch of ground nutmeg

1 cup [240 ml] whole milk

1 cup [240 ml] heavy cream

½ cup [120 ml] buttermilk, sour cream, or plain Greek yogurt

1) Butter a 2½-qt [2.4-L] soufflé dish and place half of the biscuit chunks in the dish. Scatter half of the cheese evenly over the biscuits. Layer the remaining biscuits on top of the cheese, and top with the remaining cheese.

2) In a large bowl, using a handheld mixer fitted with the whisk beaters or in the bowl of a stand mixer fitted with the whisk attachment, beat the eggs, egg yolks, and salt until well blended and frothy. Add the pepper, garlic powder, thyme, and nutmeg and beat until combined. Pour in the milk, cream, and buttermilk and beat until thoroughly blended.

3) Pour the egg mixture into the prepared soufflé dish, pressing gently with your hands to make sure the custard soaks all of the biscuits and coats the cheese. Cover tightly with foil or plastic wrap and refrigerate for at least 1 hour, or up to 2 days.

4) Preheat the oven to 350°F [180°C]. Remove the cover from the soufflé dish and place it in a larger pan with sides tall enough to come at least halfway up the sides of the soufflé dish. Place the pan, with the soufflé dish inside, in the oven and then pour enough scalding hot water (the hottest water from your tap is fine) into the pan so that it reaches halfway up the sides of the soufflé dish.

5) Bake until the top is lightly browned and the custard is just set, or an instant-read thermometer inserted into the center of the strata registers 160°F [70°C], about 1 hour.

6) Remove from the oven and let cool for 10 minutes. Serve warm.

NOTE: You can substitute almost any kind of bread for the biscuits; just make sure the bread is slightly stale. If you are using fresh bread, tear about 4 slices into 1-in [2.5-cm] chunks and toast the chunks on a baking sheet in a preheated 300°F [150°C] oven for 10 minutes while prepping your other ingredients.

BUTTERS
AND SPREADS

MMMMM!

MMM!!

GOOD!

STRAWBERRY BUTTER

MAKES ABOUT 1 CUP [260 G]

Bright pink with flecks of red, a little sweet but not too much—Strawberry Butter is pretty to look at, fun to eat, and ridiculously easy to make. Choose berries that are ripe—deep red, sweet, and fragrant—but don't worry about what they look like, because they'll be puréed into the butter. It's important that your butter and berries *both* be at room temperature so that the butter will whip up properly; if the berries are cold, then the butter will solidify and resist whipping.

1 cup [120 g] whole fresh or frozen strawberries, at room temperature

½ cup [110 g] salted butter, at room temperature

¼ cup [30 g] confectioners' sugar

1) Slice the tops with the stems off the fresh strawberries and discard. Cut the strawberries into quarters and then mash them with the back of a spoon or a potato masher until just a few chunks remain. (Alternatively, in the bowl of a food processor fitted with the metal blade, process the berries for about 10 seconds.)

2) In the bowl of a stand mixer fitted with the whisk attachment, whisk together the butter, berries, and sugar at medium speed until very smooth and light, about 3 minutes. (Alternatively, in a medium bowl with a wire whisk, beat by hand until light and fluffy, 3 to 5 minutes.)

3) Serve immediately or store, tightly covered, in the refrigerator for up to 1 week or in the freezer for up to 1 month. Can be served cold, or let soften at room temperature for 20 minutes before serving.

 *Variations*

Peach Butter: Substitute 1 small ripe peach, peeled, pitted, and cut into ½-in [12-mm] chunks, for the strawberries.

Raspberry Butter: Substitute 1 cup [120 g] fresh or frozen (thaw before using) ripe raspberries for the strawberries.

HONEY BUTTER

MAKES 5/8 CUP [130 G]

Creamy and smooth and not too sweet, honey butter makes everything better. Smear it on biscuits or top a waffle or a stack of pancakes with a good-size pat to make breakfast just a little more special.

½ cup [110 g] salted butter, at room temperature

2 Tbsp honey

In the bowl of a stand mixer fitted with the whisk attachment or in a medium bowl with a wire whisk, whisk the butter and honey together until very smooth and light, about 1 minute. Serve immediately or store, tightly covered, in the refrigerator for up to 2 weeks or in the freezer for up to 1 month. Can be served cold, or let soften at room temperature for 20 minutes before serving.

 *Variations*

Maple Butter: Substitute pure Grade B maple syrup for the honey.

Molasses Butter: Substitute dark molasses for the honey.

GARLIC HERB BUTTER

MAKES ⅝ CUP [130 G]

Garlic Herb Butter is an easy, versatile way to liven up your cooking and baking. As a spread for savory muffins and biscuits, it can't be beat. I like to whip this up with whichever herbs are growing in the garden (or languishing in the vegetable drawer of the fridge) and slather it on any of the plain biscuits in this book. Any extra can be used to dress up baked or sautéed fish or roasted chicken, or used to make the best garlic bread you've ever had.

½ cup [110 g] salted butter, at room temperature

1 garlic clove, minced

2 tsp minced fresh flat-leaf parsley or 1 tsp dried parsley, rubbed between your fingers to crush

1 tsp minced fresh tarragon or ½ tsp dried tarragon, rubbed between your fingers to crush

1 tsp minced fresh thyme or ½ tsp dried thyme, rubbed between your fingers to crush

1 tsp minced fresh sage leaves or ½ tsp dried sage, rubbed between your fingers to crush

In a medium bowl, combine the butter, garlic, parsley, tarragon, thyme, and sage leaves and stir with a wooden or plastic spoon for about 1 minute, or until thoroughly combined. Store, tightly covered, in the refrigerator for up to 2 weeks or in the freezer for up to 1 month. Can be served cold, or let soften at room temperature for 20 minutes before serving.

 *Variations*

Rosemary Garlic Butter: Substitute 1 Tbsp minced fresh rosemary (or 1½ tsp minced dried rosemary) for the parsley, tarragon, thyme, and sage.

Lemon-Parsley Garlic Butter: Substitute 2 tsp lemon zest for the tarragon, thyme, and sage.

MEYER LEMON CURD

MAKES ABOUT ⅔ CUP [150 G]

Meyer lemons, available in the winter months, are a little sweeter and more fragrant than regular Eureka lemons, and they're divine in a traditional lemon curd. In case you were under the impression that fresh homemade lemon curd was a complicated affair involving double boilers, thermometers, and other equipment, let me draw your attention to what is likely an underutilized appliance in your kitchen: your microwave. You can whip up a batch of tart, delicious, homemade curd using nothing more than a bowl, a whisk, and your microwave in the time it takes the biscuits to bake; it's really that fast and easy. If you want to substitute regular (Eureka) lemons, increase the sugar by 2 tablespoons. If your curd seems slightly grainy after refrigerating, don't worry; it's just tiny bits of butter. Let your curd warm to room temperature before serving, and it will be smooth as silk.

½ lb [230 g] Meyer lemons

3 Tbsp salted butter, melted and slightly cooled

1 egg

¼ cup [50 g] sugar

1) Using a fine grater (I recommend a microplane-style grater), zest the lemons, being careful to remove just the rind and not the white pith, which is bitter. Then cut the lemons crosswise in half and juice them, straining out any seeds. You should have about ¾ cup [180 ml] lemon juice.

2) In a medium microwave-safe mixing bowl, whisk together the melted butter, the egg, and the sugar, then add the lemon juice and zest and whisk until thoroughly combined. Microwave at 50 percent power in 1-minute increments, whisking the curd and scraping down the bowl after each minute, for a total of 5 minutes, or until the curd has thickened slightly (it will coat the back of a spoon), the color has slightly darkened, and the curd looks more translucent. Don't worry if it seems a bit thin; it will thicken as it cools.

3) Let cool, whisking occasionally, for 5 to 10 minutes, then strain the curd through a fine-mesh strainer (use a spoon or a rubber spatula to push the curd through the strainer) held over a storage container. Discard any solids left in the strainer. Cover the curd tightly and refrigerate until fully cooled. Can be served immediately or stored in the refrigerator, tightly covered, for up to 1 week. May be frozen for up to 1 month; thaw overnight in the refrigerator before using.

CONT'D

 *Variations*

Rosemary–Meyer Lemon Curd: Add 1 tsp fresh rosemary leaves (or ½ tsp dried) with the zest. This variation is particularly delicious on fresh biscuits.

Passion Fruit Curd: Substitute ⅓ cup [80 ml] fresh passion fruit pulp for the lemon juice and zest.

Lime Curd: Substitute ½ lb [230 g] limes for the Meyer lemons, and increase the sugar by 1 Tbsp.

Raspberry Curd: In the bowl of a food processor fitted with the metal blade or in a blender, purée ½ cup [60 g] fresh or frozen (and thawed) rasp-berries. Strain through a fine-mesh strainer, then fold the purée into the cooled Meyer Lemon Curd.

FIG *AND* ORANGE CHUTNEY

MAKES ABOUT 3 CUPS [720 ML]

This recipe is courtesy of my good friend and chutney maker extraordinaire Alison McQuade of McQuade's Celtic Chutneys. We have used her sweet-'n'-sour fruit chutneys in our grilled cheese sandwiches, and I have become particularly fond of her fig chutneys; they're fantastic slathered on fresh biscuits.

8 oz [230 g] dried figs, stems removed and chopped into ¼-in [6-mm] pieces (Mission and Calimyrna figs are good choices)

2 cups [480 ml] hot water

1 large sweet orange, such as a Valencia or navel

½ cup [100 g] firmly packed brown sugar

½ cup [120 ml] apple cider vinegar (preferably unfiltered)

⅔ cup [90 g] raisins

½ tsp kosher salt

¾ tsp ground ginger

¼ tsp ground allspice

¼ tsp ground cloves

¼ tsp ground nutmeg

¼ tsp cayenne

Pinch of freshly ground black pepper

1) In a medium bowl, soak the fig pieces in the hot water until the figs are soft, about 30 minutes. Strain, reserving ½ cup [120 ml] soaking water. Transfer the softened figs and the reserved soaking water to a medium nonreactive saucepan.

2) Using a microplane-style grater or the smallest holes on a box grater, grate the zest from the orange, being careful to avoid the bitter white pith. (Alternatively, remove the zest in strips with a vegetable peeler and then chop finely.) Cut a slice off the top and bottom of the orange, stand the orange on one cut end, and carefully cut the remaining pith and outer layer of membrane off the orange, leaving the segments exposed. Working over a medium bowl to catch any released juice, use your hands (or a small knife if the segments will not easily release) to remove all of the orange segments, separating them from the membrane and seeds. Chop the segments into ½-in [12-mm] chunks and add the orange chunks, any juice that has been released, and the zest to the saucepan with the figs.

CONT'D

3) Add the brown sugar, apple cider vinegar, raisins, salt, ginger, allspice, cloves, nutmeg, and cayenne to the figs and stir with a wooden spoon or plastic spatula to combine. Bring to a boil over medium heat, turn the heat to low, and simmer, stirring occasionally, for 30 minutes. The mixture should thicken and darken, but if the mixture begins to stick to the pan, add extra soaking water, 2 Tbsp at a time, just until the mixture is no longer sticking and has enough liquid to maintain a simmer.

4) Let cool in the pan for 10 minutes and then transfer the chutney to a heat-safe nonreactive container, cover, and cool completely in the refrigerator. Store in a resealable container in the refrigerator for up to 1 month.

BROWN SUGAR–BOURBON SAUCE

MAKES ABOUT 1 CUP [240 ML]

We serve this incredibly easy and delicious dessert sauce on our bread pudding, and it's also a key part of Individual Monkey Bread (page 139). If you wind up with extra, drizzle it over ice cream, cheesecake, pancakes, or waffles for a sophisticated treat. Make this sauce your own! Instead of bourbon, feel free to substitute rum, rye, amaretto, orange liqueur, or applejack (apple brandy).

½ cup [100 g] packed dark brown sugar

¼ cup [55 g] salted butter, at room temperature

¼ cup [60 ml] heavy cream

1 Tbsp bourbon

1 tsp vanilla extract

1) In a small saucepan over medium-low heat, melt the sugar and butter together, whisking constantly until smooth.

2) Turn the heat to low and carefully add the cream, bourbon, and vanilla (the mixture may boil up at this point, so add the liquids slowly and keep whisking constantly). Bring the sauce to a simmer and cook for 5 minutes, whisking occasionally, or until slightly thickened.

3) Remove from the heat and let cool for 5 to 10 minutes before using. Store in a resealable container in the refrigerator for up to 1 month. Warm in a microwave when you're ready to serve.

TANGERINE-VANILLA BEAN MARMALADE

MAKES 1 QT [960 ML]

We serve a piece of fresh seasonal fruit with all of our grilled cheese sandwiches at The American Grilled Cheese Kitchen: strawberries in the spring, stone fruit in the summer, apples in the fall, and tangerines in the winter. We go through cases of fruit a day at each store, and the not-quite-perfect fruit is either donated to a local food bank or turned into preserves. This marmalade is particularly good in Peanut Butter and Jelly Muffins (page 63) or just spooned onto fresh hot biscuits.

2 lb [910 g] tangerines

1 lemon

1 qt [960 ml] water, at room temperature

1 vanilla bean

4 cups [800 g] sugar

1) Put two small ceramic plates or saucers in the freezer; you'll need these later to check if your marmalade is done.

2) Put the tangerines and the lemon in a large, heavy-bottomed, nonreactive saucepan. Pour in the room-temperature water, adding more if necessary to just cover the fruit. (Don't worry about adding too much water; it will boil off when the marmalade is cooking.) Bring to a boil over medium-high heat.

Turn the heat to medium-low, and simmer, partially covered, until the skin of the fruit is easily pierced with a fork, about 45 minutes. Using tongs, transfer the citrus fruit to a cutting board. Reserve the cooking liquid in the saucepan.

3) When the citrus fruit has cooled enough to be easily handled (about 15 minutes), peel off the skin in about 1-in- [2.5-cm-] wide strips. With three or four strips stacked together, cut the peel into ⅛-in- [3-mm-] wide slivers. Add all of the peel to the reserved cooking liquid. Cut all the fruit in half crosswise and carefully remove all of the seeds. Place the seeds on a 6-in [15-cm] square of cheesecloth, knot together opposite corners of the square to make a small tight bundle, and add it to the cooking liquid. Chop the remaining fruit pulp into approximately ¼-in [6-mm] chunks, discarding any strands of white pith or clumps of membrane that are released in the chopped fruit. Add the chopped pulp to the cooking liquid.

4) With a small, sharp knife, split the vanilla bean lengthwise, then crosswise. Use a small spoon to scrape the seeds from the inside of the bean and add the seeds and bean pieces to the cooking liquid and peels. Stir the mixture, cover with a lid, and let sit at room temperature for at least 8 hours and up to 24 hours.

CONT'D

5) Remove the lid and bring the contents of the saucepan to a boil over medium heat. Turn the heat to medium-low and bring the mixture to a simmer. Stirring continuously with a wooden spoon or silicone spatula, add the sugar in a slow, steady stream. Keep the mixture at a gentle simmer rather than a rolling boil, adjusting the heat accordingly, and cook, stirring occasionally, until the mixture thickens and becomes translucent, about 30 minutes. To check if your marmalade will set, remove one of the plates from the freezer and drop a teaspoon of marmalade on the plate. Wait 2 minutes for it to cool and then push your finger through the puddle on the plate. If the surface of the marmalade retains wrinkles, or if the marmalade is thick and a bit gelatinous, it is done. If the puddle is watery and closes right up after your finger draws through, then keep cooking and try again after simmering for 5 minutes more. (Alternatively, if you have a candy thermometer, the marmalade is done when the temperature reaches 220°F [104°C].)

6) Allow the marmalade to cool in the pan for about 10 minutes. Using a spoon, remove the cheesecloth bundle and squeeze as much juice out of it as you can by pressing it against the side of the pan with the back of the spoon, then discard. Carefully spoon the marmalade into a glass container with a tightly fitting lid and cool completely in the refrigerator before serving. The marmalade will keep for 1 month in the refrigerator.

FRESH STRAWBERRY PRESERVES

MAKES ABOUT 1 QT [960 ML]

Use the ripest, most fragrant strawberries you can find; the flavor of the strawberries is what determines how delicious the preserves will be. It doesn't matter what the berries look like, of course, and there's no need to trim off soft or bruised spots. The lemon adds acidity and brightness, and the lemon seeds are a great source of pectin, which helps the preserves thicken and set.

1 lemon

3 cups [600 g] sugar

1¼ lb [570 g] fresh ripe strawberries, hulled and quartered

1) Put two small ceramic plates or saucers in the freezer; you'll need these later to check if your preserves are done.

2) Zest and juice the lemon, carefully removing and reserving the seeds after juicing. In a medium, heavy-bottomed, nonreactive saucepan, combine the zest, juice, and sugar.

3) Place the seeds on a 6-in [15-cm] square of cheesecloth, knot together opposite corners of the cheesecloth square to make a small tight bundle, and add the bundle to the saucepan.

4) Using a wooden or silicone spoon or spatula, stir the lemon mixture and bring to a simmer over low heat. Cook, stirring occasionally, until the sugar is fully melted, about 10 minutes.

5) Stir in the strawberries and continue cooking over low heat, stirring occasionally, until the mixture thickens and becomes translucent, about 20 minutes. If any whitish scum forms on top of the preserves while cooking, carefully skim it off with a shallow spoon and discard. To check if your preserves will set, remove one of the plates from the freezer and drop a teaspoon of preserves on the plate. Wait 2 minutes for it to cool and then run your finger through the puddle on the plate. If the surface of the preserves retains wrinkles or if the preserves are thick and a bit gelatinous, they are done. If the puddle is watery and closes right up after your finger draws through, then keep cooking and try again after simmering for 5 minutes more. (Alternatively, if you have a candy thermometer, the preserves are done when the temperature reaches 220°F [104°C].)

CONT'D

6) Allow the preserves to cool in the pan for about 10 minutes and then use a spoon to find and remove the cheesecloth package. Squeeze as much juice out of the cheesecloth as you can by pressing it against the side of the pan with the back of the spoon, then discard. Carefully pour the preserves into a glass container with a tightly fitting lid and cool completely in the refrigerator before serving. The preserves will keep for 1 month in the refrigerator.

Variation

Balsamic Vinegar and Black Pepper–Strawberry Preserves: Omit the lemon. In the saucepan, combine ⅓ cup [80 ml] of the highest-quality balsamic vinegar, ¾ tsp coarsely ground black pepper, the sugar, and the strawberries and begin at Step 5. This variation is particularly delicious spooned over vanilla ice cream.

INDEX

ACKNOWLEDGMENTS

First and foremost, I'd like to thank my husband and business partner, Nate Pollak, whose support and encouragement enabled me to write this book. He should write his own book about whatever Zen meditation practice he's taken up that has enabled him to endure my muttering about grams of butter and whether or not the apples should be peeled in addition to my having turned our home kitchen into a biscuit test lab for several months. He somehow intuited when I needed a break from baking, taking me to my favorite sushi spot for a night out, and I always knew I had a winner when he would take a bite from a warm muffin or biscuit I'd place in front of him and nod, saying, "This one's good."

Mom, thanks for letting me spill honey and melted butter all over your cookbooks when I was seven and for not getting upset that time I tried to make puff pastry by hand when I was ten.

Another reason why I wrote this second book was for the chance to work on a photo shoot once again with Antonis Achilleos and Vanessa Dina. How these two professionals make hot melted cheese look so amazing while standing outdoors in the windy cold of San Francisco mystifies and astounds me. To the warm and enthusiastic crew at Chronicle Books, thank you, thank you, and thank you again for taking a risk on me, supporting me, and not thinking it's weird that I drop off random baked goods at your office. Amy Treadwell, Amy Cleary, Doug Ogan, Sara Golski, Tera Killip, Steve Kim . . . and everyone I'm missing.

Ethan Speizer, thank you for giving up your weekend to bake with me for the photo shoot. And to all my tasters and testers, who gamely tried a recipe or a result and gave me feedback: I couldn't have done it without you. I'm looking at you, Jamie Hansen, Diana Reed, BFFs Dave and Andrea, Scout Addis, my adorable neighbors Jeannie and Amy, the nice folks at Mission Cliffs rock climbing gym, and especially the entire staff of ChefsFeed. Daniel, thank you for believing in me even when I don't. Oh! I can't forget my state-of-the-art organic energy-starred composting and cleaning crew, Mickey and Tilly. Good job, team.